LITTLE LORRAINE

The horrific true story of one child's journey
from hell and her 30 year battle for justice

by

EDWARD WHITE

ISBN: 9798521587483

StoryKinds 7750 Okeechobee Boulevard,
Suite 4-633,
West Palm Beach, FL 33414

www.justiceforlorraine.com

First eBook Edition: July 2021

Dedication

To my husband and 5 beautiful children.
It has been a privilege to have you all in my life
and to my co-writer, thank you.

Contents

FOREWORD

Systemic abuse within our society contains structures, primarily designed to control individuals or manipulate them for material or political gain. Most social systems contain at least one structure that is self-perpetuating and actively discourages reporting. These structures, when allowed to promulgate, create a cycle of abuse that is repetitive or contagious and only leads to further pain for those attempting to seek justice.

People may not even realise they are a victim of this abuse. Sometimes it is so subtle, they end up defeating the victim using obfuscation and denial.

Resilience and perseverance are among the key strengths needed to breakthrough these barriers of corruption. Lorraine is one of many victims failed by a system that promotes the notion of trust. When we disclose these crimes, a more robust response is needed. Victims like Lorraine are a measure of our society's health. Until the authorities recognise these as more than just system failures – and hold individuals responsible to account – then nothing will change.

We have a moral obligation as a community to ensure these failures do not keep punishing the victim. Lorraine's abuser has more protection in law than she has at this moment. These paradoxical failures have only one function. To deny victims a voice and ultimately justice. If we are not speaking out against these crimes, we are complicit. We are no better than the people who facilitated the abuse in family homes and remained silent. Lorraine is not only a survivor but a warrior in her own right. Her campaign for justice has cast a light on some of the most heinous crimes any child can suffer; horrific rape and abuse. Well done Lorraine, you are a beacon of light for many victims.

Saoirse Rae

PROLOGUE

The street in front of our house was always full of kids, and as I listened to their sound of laughter I waited nervously upstairs for the front door to close. I dreaded that sound. The front door slamming always sent a rush of cold air up the stairs and froze the blood in my veins. That sound could only mean one thing. Mammy and daddy had gone and the monster was on the prowl.

AUTHOR'S NOTE

Everyone has the right to tell their story and for reasons about to be disclosed, Lorraine is telling hers. Everything you are about to read is true. Names have been changed in order to protect the privacy of certain individuals but the details remain the same.

HOUSE of HORRORS

I was born in a sleepy little town in Offaly, on the 7th June 1975, the second eldest of five sisters and two brothers. The house where I grew up was so was small if you wanted to change your mind you had to step outside.

Built in the 1940s, it was one of several two-up, two-down council houses where everybody in the street knew each other. The furniture was sparse, and the house looked and smelled like it had gone on fire and was never rebuilt. Upstairs was the worst. The rooms were like prison cells. Children occupied most of what little space was left available, and during the winter months, we huddled together for warmth.

Our beds were never clean, and neither were we. Years of baked in grime and grease made living conditions unbearable. It could take a month of scrubbing with Brillo pads to get to the stage where you could say, 'sorry about the mess!'

Everywhere there were handprints covered in mould.

There was so much filth and decay it became part of the decor. Around the back of the house, rubbish was strewn about and bits of old bikes and paint pots doubled up as urinals or ashtrays.

A pile of dirty laundry was as good a seat as any and socks became mittens. You were always stepping in something foul and your shoes stuck to the floor. There were lots of creepy things living upstairs, but some of those had hands.

None of the children washed. The safest place to hide money was under the soap. I remember we put a Christmas tree up once but it wilted within a half an hour. During the winter, the house was so cold; we used to put the milk in the fridge to stop it from freezing.

From a very early age, I knew my parents were odd. Nobody much visited them because nobody was ever invited. Whenever I visited my friend's houses I used to wonder how their rooms were always kept so clean? The linen in their houses smelt so fresh and they had lots of nice things in their bathrooms I had never seen before.

Their towels were always so fluffy, but we had none and you'd half expect their toilet to cough before it flushed. Some of their loos had posh things hanging off the edge of the bowl and the water used to turn a lovely shade of blue. That fascinated me no end. I'd wait for the water to fill back up to flush it again. Anyone listening downstairs must have thought I had the scutters with the number of times I pressed the handle.

I'd never seen bath salts before either. One time I stuck my tongue in one to see what it was like. I got a fright when it started to fizzle, and for a second I thought I'd poisoned myself.

There seemed to be such a big difference between how they lived and how we lived, it made me feel sad.

These weren't rich people on the street that I grew up on. They were just ordinary hard-working folk that made the best of what they had. Their homes were immaculate compared to ours, and I couldn't help but feel our family was from a different planet.

Our parents kept themselves to themselves. They had way too many secrets to allow anybody get too close. Those that did, never hung around for very long.

Most of my friends thought mammy was mental, but so did we, so that was grand. She could start a fight with herself in a mirror, and if she wasn't screaming at the kids, the neighbours dogs were attacking her.

For years, I thought my first name was, 'here you!'

"What the fook is wrong with her now?" was a regular thing you'd hear from all the neighbours.

"Ya better not be tormenting them children or I'll come through that door and bate the fookin' head'o'ya!" said one.

"The smell in that house would knock a fly off a bucket of shite!" Mrs Hannigan used to say.

And she was right! It was the first thing to hit you, and your gag reflex never really got used to it.

Our house was the smelliest in Birr and I'm not ashamed to admit it. It was full of filth, shit, and piss, and if that didn't knock you for six, the smell off mammy would.

She washed herself once a month whether or not she needed to, and her pig of a son was the same. They were pure filthy. The stink was woeful; they could rob a bank just threatening to stand beside you. This wasn't that everyday sweaty smell that you get with some people; it was much worse than that.

It was like they were rotten to the core and I used to wonder, was this why the social workers never stayed around for very long? Was mammy using stink warfare to keep everyone away?

They nailed shut the upstairs windows in our house so

the smell couldn't escape and neither could the flies. Nothing survived for more than half an hour in our house. If it moved or blinked mammy either ate it or my brother interfered with it. Mammy used to say, "if it still has feelings it isn't cooked enough," and it was true. Often times we'd see things running around the kitchen floor with mammy chasing after it, but we never knew if she cooked whatever was caught?

We didn't have a TV in the early days. We used to sit and watch the fire go out until someone put more coal on it. There was no question of bringing friends upstairs. If the bottom half of the house didn't choke the head off you, the upstairs would. That's where all the worst smells were.

Even the conversation was mouldy. Whenever anyone spoke, mammy and daddy would cut across them and always interrupt. The conversation had to revolve around them and if you were still listening after thirty minutes of that; you were either unconscious or deaf. My mother had a fan-belt on her mouth and she used to get a cramp in her face from talking. You knew by the look of her she was pure thick, but dare you tell her? Daddy secretly hated her, but just hadn't the balls to say so. There was never any intimacy between them. How could there be? If you rubbed mammy the wrong way, she'd immediately lose the head. She'd clatter you so hard, your kids would be born dizzy. You couldn't get close to her. She was as mad as a bag of cats. We used to wonder how she got pregnant, and so did all the neighbours.

"Ya couldn't be going near any of that," says one.

"I know, sure, but how could he?"

"Would you be well?"

"Jazuz, you couldn't be?"

"Must have been artificial insinuation?"

"Artificial what...?"

"You know that thing the vets do to make a cow pregnant?"

"Oh, that!?"

"Yeah, Stella'd be mad up for that!"

"I tell you now girls, a vet would be in and out of there fairly handy like?"

"Sure, look at the cut of her?"

"I know, you'd get a bad 'oul dose!"

"I swear to fook, if beauty is skin deep, that 'wan has to be inside out?

"Is right!"

"I tell yee now, if that fella didn't toss and turn in the

bed, there'd be no children in that house at all?"

"Was he even there for the birth of her last child?"

"I don't think he was even there for the making of it?"

"Sure her mother was the same as her mother before her.

She used to throw the kids up in the air and walk away!"

"Oh, she never did?"

"Oh, she did, is right!"

"Rumour has it, himself died from the drink?"

"Is that right?"

"Didn't yer 'wan come home mad with the drink one night and shoot him?"

"Isn't that, shocking?"

"But Lord, save us tonight, that house of theirs is shockin' damp!"

"What d'ye think of me new tan, she says to me?"

"That's not a fookin' tan, says I, that's rust!"

The neighbours could keep that up all day and you'd have a pain in your side from laughing. They were always making a laugh or a joke to keep us cheered up. I don't know what I would have done without them. Whenever mammy and daddy went shopping, daddy would slip a few cans of cider into the basket and mammy would say to him at the top of her voice, "we

can't afford dem ya big fookin' eejit," and make a holy
show of him in the shop.

Ten minutes later she's putting lipstick in the basket and
daddy says, "what's that shit for?"

"That's to make me look beautiful?" she'd say.

"And what do you think the cans are for?" says daddy.
Next thing, another big row would kick-off and she'd
call him a 'cunt' all the way up the street before stopping for a piss behind a hedge. Mammy's language was a
terror, but she'd pee anywhere. She didn't care, and
she'd leave you mortified.

My aunt Breda used to say, 'there's no such thing as
monsters,' but I wasn't so sure. I figured there were at
least three of the fecker's living in our house. The Divil
himself wouldn't have put up with them. There were
horrible people living in our house, and the signs of
torment were all there if anyone bothered to look.
When I was about 12-years-old, I remember being
asked by the school doctor, "does your urine burn?" I
said, "I don't know, mammy never put a match to it?"
The doctor said, "no Lorraine, that's not what I
meant?"

I said, "I don't understand? Mammy burns everything in
our house, but I never seen her burn anything like

16

that?"

"Do you have trouble passing water, is what I mean?"

"Yeah, I suppose I get a bit scared going over a bridge sometimes? My sister nearly drowned in the river Brosna? I said, looking at him tongue-in-cheek.

He looked back at me and smiled. I knew what he was getting at. All the signs I was being abused were there, and he didn't have to dig too deep to find out.

I just wasn't able to tell him what was happening because I was scared. But that's the first question that needs to be asked? Denial is very common in abused children talking about things like bruising down below, but I managed to get around those questions every time. With so many children to see in one school, there was never time to ask the right questions, and that's all they needed to do.

Nowadays, medical staff and teachers are much better equipped to spot the signs of abuse, but not when I was growing up. None of us ever got properly examined and who knows how many other victims there were?

JESUS, MARY & JOSEPH

When I eventually found the strength to write this book, it was like a two-ton weight had lifted off my shoulders. And not just for me, but for my entire family.

For years, I had been hiding the truth. Not only from them, but myself included. Nobody could understand the mood swings or why I suddenly got depressed for no obvious reason. My past was affecting everyone I loved and cared about; and in ways I never imagined. They deserved better, and I owed them an explanation. I was fed up living a lie, but where do you start with something like this? The beginning, I suppose?

As a child, I never talked about bad stuff. It was safer that way. The only time my parents ever listened to me was when social workers were about, but other than that, they ignored me. Instead of asking for attention or a hug, there had to be something physically wrong with you. But it had to be serious? Things like a broken leg or bleeding to death might get you noticed, but not if it was dinner time or going to the pub. You may stay where you are. With so many children all vying for attention, the most basic needs of a child, such as being fed, loved, cared about, were low priorities.

We were always hungry. I can never remember a time when we weren't. Finding food was the one thing that occupied a lot of our spare time. The search was endless, and while I wouldn't go as far as to say we were starving, there was never enough to go around. And there was a reason for that. My mother and father were never out of the pub. The children's allowance was spent on booze. They went drinking every night. They'd leave the house at about 7 or 8 o'clock each night and wouldn't come home until closing time. That was their routine. They'd leave us with nothing to eat and a slice of toast was supper before bed. You couldn't have a bowl of Weetabix because mammy used to count them, and woe betide if she found any crumbs in the bed. Sometimes there was nothing at all to eat, and that was nearly all the time. The nagging pain of hunger made it difficult to get to sleep and drinking water helped a bit. But that only made you want to pee, and then you'd be back to being hungry again.

During the day, the house was like a zoo. Children were

running about in sodden nappies and those that had none just went to the toilet where they stood. Mammy never bothered to clean up the mess and would wait for daddy to come home after work to do it instead.

One neighbour made the mistake of mentioning the smell of piss in our house, and how terrible it was that none of us kids were potty trained. She was perfectly right, but when mammy heard this, she threw a fit.

"That one can mind her own fookin' business, I can tell you now! Who's she to tell me how to run my home? I'll deal with my kids as I fookin' like an' what harm is there in a little bit of piss? Sure it never bothered nobody in this fookin' house?"

It bothered us a lot! Mammy was a filthy article, and that's being polite. The smell of urine all over the house was suffocating, and especially during the summer months. The stink was everywhere and smelled like one big toilet. You could never get used to that type of smell. It was stale urine on top of rotten everything else, and you couldn't wait to get outside and play.

Mammy took no pride in herself, her children, or her home. To her, children were just a nuisance. She treated them as an irritation. We always seemed to be in her way, and there was no question of running to her for a hug. She was repulsive. Her nails were filthy, and she had scraggly hair that was greasy and unkempt. She just wandered around the house as if none of us existed. We were just mouths to feed, and it was much safer to stay out of her way. If there was such a thing as a wicked witch, mammy would have boiled us all in a pot. She had zero maternal instincts and when a new baby arrived in the house; it was up to all of us to raise it. She only ever gave birth and knowing her, she would have had somebody else to do that for her, too.

I thought at one stage we were breastfed by our father. He always had a bottle in his hand in the early days. There was no such thing as bonding in her mind. Mammy wanted the new-born raised as quickly as possible and out of her hair. She had much more important things to do, like eating and drinking or having affairs. She had no other interests apart from gossip. Mammy loved to tear people apart. She had a persecution complex and was convinced everyone was out to get her. And she was half right; they were!

She had every reason to feel paranoid. Her antics down the pub, were legendary, and it didn't take her long to get a name for herself. She would regularly pick fights while drunk and never stopped to think about what she said to anyone.

Stella, the 'mad one' as she was known, was despised up and down our road. You didn't so much as talk to mammy, as tolerate her.

Daddy, on the other hand, was much more reserved, but devious to the bone. We used to wonder what the two of them ever saw in each. None of us could figure it out, but that wasn't a safe topic of conversation.

Any criticism of mammy or daddy was severely punished. She'd murder you if she found out you were talking about her behind her back. There was no question of her having any flaws. Any criticism of mammy came mostly from the neighbours who hated her with a passion. They were well used to her foul-mouthed rants. Mammy's language was the first thing you'd hear in the morning and the last thing at night. If she wasn't cursing up and down the street, she was pissing in someone's garden. Even the dogs crossed to the other side of the road when they saw her coming.

Aunt Breda used to say, "if that bitch came to visit my house, the rats would throw themselves on the traps." The rats never came near our house. They had more sense. Mammy hated animals as much as she hated the neighbours. Anything on four legs that couldn't be cooked or eaten, was chased out the door.

Her other pastime, if you can call it that, was to sit at the front window in our house and tear asunder every single neighbour that walked past. There were no exceptions, and yet if such-and-such a neighbour stopped to talk to her, she'd be all over them like a rash; once, of course, the conversation was about her. If it wasn't, she'd quickly tune out and find an excuse to walk away. "Wud ya look at the fookin' state of that one and her new flowery dress and makeup she stole from the chemist? Who does she think she fookin' is? The cut of her! And wait till I tell you about that one ridin' such-and-such. If only her husband knew?"

It was shocking the way she carried on and I thought to myself, you dirty two-faced oul' trout, how would you feel if they were talking about you that way?

Ironically enough, they were! Mammy was the talk of the street as I quickly discovered and with good reason. Social workers were in and out of our house more often than the dog. The neighbours had her spotted. There were regular complaints made about the children in our house, but that was only the tip of it.

Mammy used to curse them out of it, but every time a social worker arrived, the transformation was remarkable. Gone was the foul-mouthed oul' hag and in its place was the perfect mammy that butter wouldn't melt in her mouth. It was sickening to watch as we were all paraded into the front living room, to be questioned in turn. The social workers didn't give a hoot. We had that spotted, but dare we open our mouths to any of them about anything that went on in that house?

After a while, we made bets among ourselves to see which of them could tolerate the smell the longest. Most of them couldn't wait to get out of there and they were no more interested in how you were doing than the man on the moon. If they were really that interested, the evidence was all over the place?

We looked malnourished; we stank to high heaven; the house smelt like a sewer and every man and his dog, except them, apparently, knew we were being abused.

You didn't need a degree in rocket science to figure out what was going on. All you needed to do was take one of us aside and ask us to speak to us privately?

But you couldn't, because mammy had them sussed, and she'd glare at you if you so much as looked at any of these 'social cunts' sideways, as she called them.

I lost count of the amount of times I wanted to blurt things out, but I was terrified that if I said anything, I'd be left there to suffer the consequences. Even before any social worker would arrive, mammy had us well coached.

"Now, c'mere you," she'd say to me. "You've a big fookin' mouth on ya. If I hear you talking to one of them cunts, so help me jazuz, you better have a bus ticket in your pocket. I'll fuckin' bury ya, I swear on me mudder's grave. D'ya hear me, ya little cunt?" and she'd smack you across the side of the head just for emphasis.

Any decent social worker worth their salt could see the terror written all over our faces. This was a hostage situation. There was no possible way it was safe for us to speak up. Yet this was the scenario played out week after week in that house of horrors. I used to scream at the social workers using only my eyes, but mammy was watching everyone like a hawk for any signs of betrayal. If she sensed that any of us were trying to communicate hidden messages, the beating you got was unmerciful.

"C'mere to me now, you little cunt," she'd say, grabbing you by the hair the second the social worker was out the door.

"What did I tell you about talking to them cunts?" Bang! she'd hit you a blow to the side of the head with a shoe or a poker that she had ready in her hand.

"Maaaaa, I said nothing I'd scream back at her.

"Ya did in your fook! I saw how you were looking at that last wan' with the big sympathy head on ya! What are ya fookin' at? Are ya tryin' to get us all locked up, are ya? And then the beating would start. It didn't matter what you said next. Once she had herself convinced you'd given someone the look, that was it. She'd be dug out of you. All you could do was curl up in a ball on the floor and hope to survive the onslaught. But it was as vicious as it was painful. The cruelty was beyond anything I could describe, and nobody could make it stop except her. She literally kicked me around the floor like a football and there was no escape.

When daddy got home later that day, he'd be told I gave the social worker a look, and she'd use that as an excuse to launch another assault on top of the battering earlier.

"What did you fookin' do, Lorraine?" he'd say, looking at me standing at the top of the stairs, bruised from head to toes.

"Honest, I said nothing, daddy!" I'd say in tears. "I swear!"

"She's a lying cunt. I saw her with me own fookin' two eyes!" mammy would scream back at me beckoning me with a talon to come down the stairs.

This ordeal was so terrifying sometimes I'd wet myself with the fright. But the end result was always the same. I was only a little cunt, and I was the one who grassed on mammy, and that's why they kept coming back.

"What were the socials asking this time?" said daddy.

"She was goin' on with the usual fookin' shite and then she looks at that wan there and when she asks her is she alright? And yer wan is giving her the big lower lip and whatnot like she's been all tortured and shite?"

"I'm not putting up with that cunt in this house. You leave me with the whole fookin' lot of 'em, an' I dunno what to be saying when they do be callin'?

And then ya have that little cunt windin' her up 'n' all. I'll bate the head off ya, d'ya hear me, ye little fookin' bitch?" said mammy.

Daddy looked at me sternly and asked, "well, what have ya to say for yourself?"

"I did nothing, daddy, I swear," I said, in heaps of tears. "I was only sitting on the steps and the lady starts asking me questions and all, and I didn't know what to be saying to her," I said, in between big heaving sobs.

"She's a lying little cunt, don't mind her?" mammy screamed at daddy, "and don't ya be thinking about taking her side agin' me? I'm fookin' tellin' yee now, I won't put up with it. I've enough to be putting up with trying to rear all yee little cunts, without yee runnin' around telling tales up and down the street as well?"

"I didn't say nothing, to nobody?" I replied.

"Shut fookin' up you, who's talkin' to you? I'm doin' the talkin' here. You won't talk back to me in me own house. I've enough from those cunts down the street as it is without listenin' to the likes of you? Now, get up them fookin' stairs or I'll give ya something to cry about, d'ya hear me?" she screamed, as she smacked me across the head while I scrambled up the steps.

I hated her so, so much. I just wanted her to die. Daddy, meanwhile, just sat back in the chair and let her get on with it. He never intervened or spoke up. It was like dealing with the Devil and his wife because no decent father would allow any of that to happen?

That night, I lay in bed bruised and battered and wondered to myself, how was I still alive after that? Two beatings in the one day? If they really hated me so much; why didn't they just kill me and get this over with? Why was mammy and daddy being so mean?

It seemed so unfair, but I had no answers. And then I fell asleep. But that didn't last for very long.

Somebody was touching me again; and I knew immediately by the smell who it was?

NEAR MISS

Around the same time as my brother started abusing other girls in the locality, there was a big commotion in the house one day and none of us knew what it was about. Unbeknownst to us, the monster had been taken to court.

A 10-year-old-girl, related to a girlfriend of his, was allegedly molested by him while she was asleep. It was a dreadful assault and when the father of the child was told, he stormed down to the flat where the monster was living and dragged him up the street by the ear to the Garda station. That was a fair walk in your under-pants. But it was late at night and few people saw what happened, more is the pity. The father faced the possi-bility of being accused of assault himself, but no charges were pressed. By rights, he should have been given an award for not kicking him up the street, and he showed remarkable restraint by just walking.

However, when the case went ahead for the little girl, it

was thrown out on a technicality. She got the date of the assault mixed up under cross-examination, but it was enough for the bastard to walk free.

According to her father, she was never right for years after that, and it was another missed opportunity to put this sicko away. But again, this is where victims blame themselves when the system fails them. Getting paedophiles into court is one thing, but putting them behind bars is another. A courtroom is one of the most hostile environments for any victim, young or old, and paedophiles use that to their full advantage.

The majority of victims have never seen the inside of a courtroom, and they are lucky if they even get that far. It takes many hours of counselling and work to prepare yourself for that ordeal and few are up to the challenge. Having your personal details read out in court or being told it must have been something you said or did that caused the abuse and the case is over before it's even begun.

That's what makes it so hard for victims to come forward. And, ironically, that's exactly what my parents did to me.

It's every child's worst nightmare and is a shocking thing to do to any adult child. Even today my parents are going around the town where I used to live looking for sympathy and getting none of it.

When the monster was taken to court and got off, the pair of them went down to the pub to celebrate and left me in the house to be raped. That is a fact!

But can you imagine celebrating a victory like that, never mind what he did to me later that night?

I'd be mortified if they accused one of my boys of something like that? I'd be dug out of him and the last thing I'd do was celebrate if he got off. I'd put him in jail myself if he was accused of rape. But there's no fear of it. My sons were raised in a good home and thankfully those who know me personally know I'm not the type to go around spreading filthy rumours. You just don't do things like that in a small town. There wouldn't be a pub left in Offaly for myself and my husband to enjoy a drink cos we'd be fecked out of it and proper order, but as for that other pair?

When I found out what happened, I made a solemn vow that would never happen to me. I watched how my parents celebrated when the case was dismissed. I could see the joy on their faces when they returned home from court that day. They may as well have won the Lotto, but I didn't understand what was going on at the time.

As the details of the court case emerged, I wanted to scream at them, "do you not know he's doing that to me too?" but I never said a word. Mammy's pet monster looked at me and whispered under his breath, 'now, see what will happen to you if you try and open your mouth?'

And he was right! Fifteen minutes later, I was stretched out on that filthy floor downstairs as he tore at my underwear and violated me once more.

As I clenched my teeth, waiting for it to be over, I swore vengeance. Not just for me, but for all those who have been abused. You know who you are if you are reading this. Your abuser might have stolen your innocence, but they haven't stolen your voice.

MAY 2012

The two female Gardai sitting opposite me in the interview room looked like neither of them wanted to speak first. But I knew before they even spoke; the news was not good. I had a sixth sense for things like this and had been dreading this moment all morning. I could barely sleep the night before following the call to come into the Garda station and as I frantically searched their faces for any glimmer of hope, my heart began to sink.

For a second or two, I thought about getting up and walking out, but what was the point; I had waited over thirty years for this moment, and figured what's a few more minutes?

Not knowing how I was going to react was the hard part. There was so much at stake. I had literally put my life on hold since starting this journey. Finding the courage to make a complaint after keeping something a secret for so long was a huge leap of faith. My whole life felt like one big lie and it was only through counselling that I realised how much of a burden that was. It's a terrible drain on your energy and can lead to mental health issues and even Cancer they say, and I had several scares already.

But nothing could have prepared me for what followed next.

"Lorraine, we've examined all the evidence," one of them began slowly, "and there's a big piece of the Jigsaw puzzle missing."

I looked at her like she was speaking in slow motion.

"Does that mean what I think it means?" I said.

"There's a piece we still need to find," she said.

The mention of a jigsaw irritated me. I never liked doing those things. There always seemed to be a piece missing. Either the dog ate it or the kids lost it, or it was never in the box, but I don't remember finishing one, ever!

"We have spoken to most of your family, and they haven't done you any favours," she said, biting her lower lip.

Well, no surprises there; the Gardai hadn't done me any either, but I didn't tell her that, and shrugged.

"I think what they are trying to say is, their version of the story is very different from yours," the Garda continued.

"Which means, they're calling me a liar?" I said.

She pursed her lips and pushed her chair back from the

desk as if I was about to launch an attack.

Maybe it was the way I was looking at her, but that was the furthest thing from my mind. I'm not the type of person to get physical over anything, but I needed to pull the stuffing out of something and the chair I was sitting on had none.

"Lorraine, trust me when I say this; we believe every word you have told us, but we are up against a brick wall at this stage of the investigation."

"You're not up against any brick wall at all," I said calmly. "You're up against a bunch of lying bastards. Now if you want to call them bricks, you can, but I think the spelling is wrong?"

They looked at each other amused, and then back at me, but neither of them replied.

Not one of my family had spoken to me since this whole investigation had begun, but that's how they did things in our family. They buried it, and anyone else who told the truth given half a chance! It was obvious at this stage of the conversation, not one of my sisters had the guts to speak up, and while none of that should have come as a shock, I wasn't in the mood for sympathy.

"Not even one of them?" I said, incredibly, as I reeled

off name after name. The Guard shook her head each time.

"The lying shower of cunts!" I said to myself.

The Guard looked at me sympathetically, but I may as well have been reading out death notices from the Offaly Independent for all the good it did.

I could feel that sense of numbness you get whenever you hear bad news, but none of this was really sinking in.

Every nod of that Garda's head was like a punch to the stomach. The last time I felt that type of pain was following the loss of my first child. That was a nightmare experience.

When I was pregnant, my mother viciously assaulted me, and I suffered a miscarriage several days later.

I was 18-years-old at the time and was about to leave home to move into a flat. A silly argument developed over a duvet that quickly escalated into a tug-of-war. I wasn't letting go, and neither was she, but my mother was a violent bitch.

I never saw it coming. She mule kicked me into the tummy and the next minute, I went flying backwards and landed on my back several feet from her on the bed.

I instinctively knew the second that happened, my unborn child was in trouble. As a mother, you just feel these things. I was violently sick the following day and couldn't eat. While I could never prove with absolute certainty, the two were linked, the little child that died inside me, left a horrible scar in my mind.

I've never spoken about it until now, and I swore I would never visit my little boy's grave until this was all over. My husband erected a memorial for him, but I couldn't bring myself to visit the grave. It was too painful. Almost thirty years have passed since the loss of my child, and only now am I beginning to sift through the wreckage.

Dealing with everything that happened in that house is a slow process and it's so easy to become overwhelmed. Losing a child under any circumstances is arguably one of the most painful things any parent should have to suffer, and for that reason, we need to be careful about apportioning blame. My mother is a vile creature at the best of times, and easily one of the most disturbed people I've ever met, but I drew the line at calling her a murderer.

I'd like to believe she never intentionally set out to harm my unborn child, but there's no getting away from what she did. When she heard about the miscarriage, there was no apology, no questions asked about how I lost the child? Nothing!

Life went on as normal in her house of horrors, and the loss of our baby was brushed under the carpet as if nothing ever happened.

Back in the interview room, all the emotions around that time came flooding back. Nobody had died this time, but it felt like I had been kicked in the gut all over again.

One of the Guards, seeing my obvious distress, asked, 'was I okay and did I want a drink of water?'

"No thanks, I'm grand!" I said, but I wasn't. This assault on the truth was making me feel sick. I wanted the pain to stop.

I wanted my husband to come and tell me this was all a bad dream; that I'd wake up at any minute and everything would be okay. But that wasn't going to happen, and I knew it.

Nothing would ever be the same. My family had disowned me, and there was nothing to show for all this. I knew from the start; the odds were stacked against me, but that didn't make it any less painful. I had taken on every single one of them, and it was my word against theirs.

The Guards had warned me this might happen, but I never imagined it would be this difficult. My family had dealt me a serious body blow, but a little voice inside my head kept saying, "this isn't over, you need to keep fighting ma!"

It was like the Ghost of my dead child was speaking to me and I could hear the words in my mind as clear as day.

"They haven't beaten you. This is only the beginning," the voice kept saying, but at the time, I didn't understand what that meant? But I do now! This little boy was speaking to me from beyond the grave and I know it sounds crazy, but I've always felt guided by his presence. He used to talk to me at other times, but I put that down to my imagination.

Today, he would have been 28-years-old and there's not a day goes by that I don't think about him. He was so wanted I can't put it into words. He was our first baby and the manner in which we lost him was tragic. We were only new parents, and we were all about making plans for the future and building a family of our own. My husband never spoke about the incident, but I knew he detested my mother like nothing else on this earth.

"While I know she didn't set out to murder the child, what do you expect to happen when you kick a pregnant daughter into the stomach?" he said, and who could argue with him?

I could see the pain in his eyes. It was the same type of pain I had felt for years and it has never diminished. And I don't want it to. Losing that little boy is part of what drives me.

He deserves to be mentioned here. His life was over before he was even born and while you can never say for certain what caused his death, I'll leave that for others to decide.

But for now, I needed to put all those feelings aside and get my head around this missing piece of the Jigsaw that the Guards kept going on about.

Where do I go looking for that?

"All we can do is carry-on," said the guard, offering no explanation; "hopefully new information might come to light?"

"What kind of information was that?" I wanted to know, but all she could say was, "they've done everything they could possibly do for now and without that missing piece...?"

Oh, feck that, I didn't want to hear any more nonsense

42

about missing jigsaw pieces. I knew that getting my parents to admit to anything was next to impossible, but it completely blew me away that not one of my sisters was prepared to come forward.

My brother had been abusing us for years and I couldn't figure out how every single one of them could turn against me?

That felt like the ultimate betrayal. But why would they do this, was the question going over and over in my mind?

They had seen what had happened to us night after night and knew what had gone on in that house for years? What about our 4-year-old sister being raped? Was that a lie, too?

What about all the reports to the Guards from other girls?

I wanted to scream at the top of my voice sitting in that chair, but I just sat there, simmering with rage. I was struggling to keep it together, and my head felt like it was about to explode.

I looked at the two Guards sitting in front of me poker-faced and for a brief, crazed moment, I thought to myself; maybe, just maybe, my sisters were right?

Everything that happened was all part of some elaborate fantasy. Was that what my sisters wanted to hear? That none of these rapes took place; that it was all a product of an over-active imagination and that I had put them through this for nothing?

"They can go shite!" I said. The whole notion that I might make any of this up was just too ridiculous for words.

I had done nothing like this before in my life and was not in the habit of making things up. They knew that! I was as loyal as any sister could be, but how could they ignore all the evidence?

My eldest sister had made a statement to the Gardai which she later withdrew under pressure. We all knew about that and she argued that because we didn't support her at the time, why should she support us now? Because back then we were all terrified. And while things are very different to what they are now, even my sisters are still too scared to speak up. There's much more support for women now than there ever was, but there's nothing worse when a parent accuses you of lying.

The law in Ireland doesn't make it easy for victims of abuse either. You're almost being re-victimised all over again when they ask questions like what took you so long to come forward and why are you only telling your story now? It's that type of formulaic thinking that victims are up against. What Gardai don't seem to realise is that family and community can put enormous pressure on victims to remain silent and especially if they too are complicit. The Gardai in my case had some serious questions to answer of their own, but we'll come to those later.

My parents decision to defend the indefensible has proven to be the biggest obstacle of all. By choosing to protect a monster and call me a liar seems an incredible thing to do, but this is the type of people they are. Totally unscrupulous. And even worse, they've dragged others into this. None of that would have been necessary had they done the decent thing and come forward. There's no justification for supporting a filthy paedophile over a defenceless child?

I appreciate we were raised by two of the sickest people imaginable but it doesn't take much to figure that out? There're no lies been told in this book. Every single word of it is the truth, and the truth hurts, but that doesn't mean we should deny it.

None of us ever spoke about the abuse.. There was this large blanket of silence thrown over everything. No one person could do this on their own and even two wasn't enough. Everyone of us needed to speak up. All it took was for one to cast a shadow over what happened, and that was enough for my father.

There was no such thing as normal growing up in the house. Our parents didn't know the first thing about parenting. Children don't behave like ponies. You can't just run them around the field and then put them in a stable each night. Children have needs. We were curious little beings, and as we got older, we started to ask questions. Awkward questions, like why does mammy not play with us and why do other people's houses not smell as bad as ours? And what's wrong with our 9-year-old sister trying to have sex with other boys in the street when it happens all the time in our house?

When one of our other sister's started shoving pencils inside herself in front of several neighbours, the reaction was revulsion and shock. But not to us. She was only 5-years-old, but that sort of thing happened all the time in our house and nobody paid any heed. It was just something she did, and she may as well have stuck a finger in her ear. Thinking back on it now, it was horrific, but there were lots of really inappropriate incidents like that. Sometimes we would wander around with no underwear on because we didn't have a second pair, and the only pair we had was soaking in the sink. But again, none of this escaped the notice of the neighbours. They were appalled, and rightly so. Children going around half-naked were perfectly normal in our house but not in theirs. We didn't know what all the fuss was about? Sometimes neighbours would bring us into their house to dress us properly and mammy would get really mad when we came home with fresh underwear. She only saw it as them interfering and trying to make a show of her.

As an adult thinking back, I often used to wonder was the way I dressed somehow responsible for the monster abusing me? There's always that niggling thought in the back of your mind. Did I do something wrong to lead him on or encourage him in some way?

When I shared this thought with the co-writer of this book, his response was immediate. "Not in the slightest! It doesn't matter how you were dressed, nobody has the right to lay a hand on you. Children are innocent. They don't have the hang-ups about their bodies that adults do and modesty is something they need to learn before they step out in the world. That's supposed to be instilled by your parents. You can't molest or abuse a child just because it happens to be naked? That's not only morally corrupt, it's an outrageous offence.

In certain countries, they treat nudity as a provocation if they rape a child. But half of these characters go around on their knuckles and use trees as transport. Culturally, they are a few thousand years behind the rest of us, but the people I'm talking about allow children as young as 7-years-old to get married so your abuser would be in good company should he choose to live there. Another reason you might think the way you do about the abuse is because of the blame culture you grew up with. Neither of your parents seem to want to take responsibility for anything and they've trained their children to take all the blame.

A healthy mind recognises mistakes and is okay with issuing an apology but not those people it seems."

Around the same time as I was writing this book my eldest sister said to a former neighbour, "we all knew what went on in that house, but why couldn't she just tell her own story and not ours?" she said.

When you think about that, it sounds perfectly reasonable? You do whatever you have to do, but don't drag us into it, is what she was saying. To her, that made perfect sense, but not to me, it didn't!

Did it really matter how many children we could stop being abused by speaking up is what she was saying? And what about the ones like myself, still struggling to get justice?

While I understood her logic, there's no getting away from the fact that what happened, happened to us all. And when she says "we all knew what went on in that house," that was an admission in itself.

But what now? Let the bastard get away with it and allow a serial paedophile to continue destroying lives like it doesn't matter?

I'm lucky. I had the support of my husband, children and friends, but the same can't be said for my other sisters.

They didn't get away so lightly and she knows what the abuse has done to them. But to isolate one sister and say, you go it alone don't mind me, is not how the justice system works.

I tried that, and it didn't work. Not once, but twice! It was their word against mine every time and she knows that. She saw what this monstrous paedophile did to us; and not just witnessed it, but experienced it first-hand?

How is anyone supposed to get justice if I were to

adopt the same attitude as her? Does she have any idea how much pain these monsters have caused and the trail of destruction they have left in their wake? Broken relationships, alcoholism, suicide, breakdowns, children being taken into care, and so on?

These are all fragments of horrific abuse caused by people who should never have been allowed to have children never mind raise them.

It's at times like this that you find out who your real friends are. While I understand she was worried about the effect this might have on her personally, there's no getting away from 'what went on in that house' as she said herself.

The fact that I had to reach outside the family for support when I couldn't rely on my own is shocking, but that's how they were raised. And criticising me is all part of their destructive thinking. I won't go as far as to say they are like my parents, but they've an awful lot of growing up to do. If they want to allow other children to be abused in the community, and turn a blind eye, that's their choice, but I'm going to do everything in my power to stop that. This serial paedophile they are choosing to protect has destroyed countless lives. You can't walk down the street and say you're doing the right thing by standing by somebody like him and the same goes for my parents. They are morally corrupt people, with no sense of right or wrong. There's a narcissistic criminal mentality at work there, but butter wouldn't melt in their mouths.

Another one of my sisters told a psychiatrist in Port-laoise what her abuser did to her. Her doctor said to me at the time, "her story was believable," but I was up that same river in Egypt as everyone else.

I was looking after her at the time following her break-down and was nowhere ready to tell my own story.

I loved her to bits and especially after all she went through. I could never put her or any of them through agony like this unless there was a good reason for doing so and they would have known that. It wasn't in my nature. You don't do things like that to your sisters.

The thing is, they knew all about the other girls too, but they still told the Guards I was telling lies?

And why had none of them ever called me? It was a question only they could answer, but it needed to be asked.

If anyone made false allegations against me or any of my children, I'd be outside their door in a heartbeat, looking for answers. But not one of them gave me that courtesy.

They didn't even have the guts to lift the phone and challenge me? Instead, they cut me off and tried to punish me for betraying some mafia code of silence.

That's just another form of abuse and the Guards could only sit and nod their heads in agreement. They knew what I was saying made sense, but what could they do?

"If they were the missing piece of the jigsaw, well then feck them, they can keep it among themselves," I said.

I could feel the anger building inside me. They knew fine well I was telling the truth and as painful as it was for all of us, there was no denying what happened in that house.

It was the stuff of nightmares. Nightmares that have haunted me for over thirty years and still do to this day. My husband will tell you, I still wake up screaming some nights, and it's even more difficult for him because I do kick him to bits while asleep.

He's also a victim of that abuse, you could say. The man who I love hasn't had a decent night's sleep in years, but was too kind to tell me until recently. It broke my heart when he did and my children have suffered too. We all suffered because of this monstrous paedophile and I hope anyone reading this will realise what they are doing by remaining silent.

Another girl who I grew up with came forward after I made the decision to go public. We had been friends for years and neither of us spoke to the other about what happened. I was so shocked when she told me. She said one day he brought her to the top of the hill where the big tree was and asked her did she want to play a game? She was only 10-years-old like myself, and had no idea what kind of game he was talking about?

"He told me to lie down so we could play a game called mammy's and daddy's and so I did as I was told," she said. "I didn't know where this was going, but I thought nothing of it, so I just went along with things. Next minute, he dropped his trousers and underpants and began to kneel down towards me, but I immediately jumped up with the fright. I had never seen anything like that before and I ran back down the hill as fast as I could. I was so scared he might run after me and catch up that I didn't dare look back." she said.

I have changed the names for legal reasons but that's all. Everything else I've written here is the absolute truth. As children, we were subjected to the most horrific sexual abuse, day in, day out. And there was no let-up. They can't deny any of that. If lying is their way of coping well, then so be it. But they have to live with the thought that every time our parents walked out that front door we went through hell. Hell, that no child on this earth should ever have to suffer.

Any sense of loyalty my sisters have towards my parents is horribly misplaced.

As I spoke, rivers of tears flowed in that interview room. My parents are psychopaths," I said. Filthy, low-life, degenerate alcoholics, who don't give a damn about anyone except themselves. Drink was their religion, and we were their slaves. They drank seven nights a week on the back of the children's allowance. That's the world these monsters inhabited. A debauched lifestyle where children were seen and not heard and abused like rag dolls.

When a local priest told me to have nothing to do with them, I couldn't believe my ears. "Just throw the thought of them in the fire and be rid of them," he said.

One of my sisters had told him the full story but he didn't want to name her or disclose any details, and I respected that. Her case didn't go ahead for whatever reason, but that's all he could say. He suspected I already knew who she was, but this was just another lurid example of the depravity going on in that house.

One Guard wanted to know did anything happen between myself and my father, but all I could say was, no!
That was the truth, as far as I could recall, but this line
of questioning stunned me. The suggestion that daddy
might be doing something like that to any of us was difficult to take in, but it was only a question.

Thinking back on it now, he was as bad as my abuser by
allowing what went on to continue. Nothing went on in
that house without him knowing, but the monster had
free rein to do as he liked.

Any decent father would have stopped what was happening immediately, but he didn't. He was more worried
about his reputation in the community than what was
happening to us children. And that was the thing that
sickened me the most. The monster was a devious bastard but so too was my father. Neither of them could
tell the truth if you set them on fire. They were expert
liars. And that's partly why all of my sisters denied
everything, too. I shouldn't have been surprised by their
refusal to tell the truth but there's always that part of
you that thinks, maybe, just maybe, one of them will do
the right thing and break the mould?

But it just goes to show what early conditioning can do

and how much control a parent can exert over an adult-child. Breaking that cycle of behaviour is one of the hardest things ever, because if I'm brutally honest, even I had been lying to myself for years.

Telling everyone I was okay when I wasn't is all part of that deception. These were not the big lies like my family were telling, these were little ones which most people call white lies.

"So how are you feeling today, Lorraine?" a friend might ask. "Ah sure, I'm grand!" I'd say, and "how's yourself?"

We all tell lies like that; but it's the really big stuff that I'm talking about here.

And it's probably why so much abuse goes unreported. The shame and the sense of guilt you feel is very difficult to cope with and I urge anyone reading this to seek help when that happens. Don't keep lying to yourself, because the longer you do, the harder it becomes to stop.

Counselling helps. Unravelling the toxic relationships that exist within families requires a lot of understanding and talking stuff out is the first step on the road to recovery.

For me, that felt a lot like emotional surgery. Some say

the emotional wounds are more painful than the physical ones, and I tend to agree with that. The abuse I suffered was so deep-rooted, the pain of that lingers to this day.

But had you asked me twenty years ago would I have done this today? I think we all know the answer to that. Therapy has been an absolute lifesaver.

The picture you have of yourself is completely at odds with how other people see you and there's a lot of growing up involved.

Children can be groomed into believing that sexual abuse is normal and one of the hardest challenges for any survivor is facing up to the pain of what they have become.

We often develop a distorted view of ourselves and our relationships. We go along with behaviour that seems perfectly normal to us, but to a normal healthy person, it's weird. And it's that distorted thinking that causes so much guilt and confusion. Sometimes it can take years to realise you've been living a lie, and for many, that knowledge often comes too late.

Divorce, alcoholism, prostitution and self-harm are all linked to childhood abuse and for some, the pain of living in that existence can be too much.

One girl the monster abused, died tragically by her own hand. She couldn't cope with what happened to her, and those are the most tragic victims of all. She was a lovely, gentle girl, and the bastard raped her mercilessly.

But it's people like her who need our help the most. We seldom get to hear their stories because they bottle it all up. When your entire family rejects you for doing nothing more than telling the truth, it's like being victimised all over again. And that's what happened to me. Sometimes I felt I couldn't take any more of the rejection, but killing myself was never an option. That's just letting the perverts win. You're only causing pain to someone else. Never do that. Go talk to someone is always the advice.

You might not be how you were before you started this journey, but have faith in the process and stick with it. If you've made it this far in the book, you can manage another few pages. It's written in a language that does away with all the psycho-babble that you frequently encounter with books of this type and for me, that's important. I hate having to Google big words, but that's all part of the learning process too and we've tried to introduce some humour as well.

THE LETTER

Some months earlier I had learned that my younger sister's children had been taken into foster care. My parents had applied for custody of her two grandchildren and they needed a letter for social services to say nothing out of the ordinary had ever happened in our home.

The monster had long since gone by that stage, so I figured my two nieces were safe enough in the house if social services monitored them. I was still in denial and with the benefit of hindsight; it was a crazy decision. It flew in the face of everything I had said about my parents in the past, but there were other forces at work which I didn't consider.

I knew my parents couldn't look after a potted plant, but the fear of my father getting angry and ignoring me was crippling. Despite all that had happened in our house, I loved my father and I didn't want to fall out with him. I still yearned for his approval but at the time I didn't realise that's a perfectly normal thing for any adult child to want and a parent could so easily take advantage of that. But it never occurred to me that if I put my signature to that letter, it might someday come back to haunt me.

I discovered later on, however, that besides the letter, two-thousand euros had been paid to each of my siblings to guarantee their silence. This only added to my sense of isolation.

I couldn't understand why my father felt the need to pay them hush money? Was I that much of a threat to him he would go to such lengths in case I changed my mind? Obviously so! My father knew I had already called the social workers to our house. And not just me, several other neighbours including my aunt Breda had reported him as well.

There was a mountain of evidence about what went on in that house, but how social services could even entertain the notion of putting two children in there was beyond me?

Clearly, I was missing something, and this bizarre request left me confused. The fact that Tusla seemed prepared to overlook what went on in that house of horrors made me question my sanity, never mind mention judgement? Had nobody bothered to speak to the Gardai? What happened to the report of my 4-year-old sister being raped? Where had that evidence got to? None of this made sense. For me, signing that letter felt like one of those false confessions you extract from prisoners of war in a hostage situation. Nobody was putting a gun to my head, admittedly, but that's how it felt. The pressure my father put me under when he brought me into the room that day was the same. I had been taught never to answer him back or question his authority and when he said jump it was always how high? I was trained like a puppy to do his bidding and be completely obedient. I felt like I had no control the moment I stepped under his roof. Even as an adult, every time I went through that door, I was back to being 8-years-old again. Had my father asked me for all the money in my purse or to sign a letter to say he was the best father in the world, I would have signed it there and then and walked out kicking myself.

He terrified me, and so did my mother. I hated when that happened, but I didn't understand the hold they had over me until many years later. It takes incredible strength of will to resist an adult who has abused you. You learned never to answer back or go against his wishes. It's how all of us were raised and it's partly why the abuse went on for so long. He had completely stripped away my boundaries, and the word 'no' didn't exist in his vocabulary. We learned children were little more than objects; something to be abused rather than nurtured and brutally punished if they stepped out of line. I lived in fear of being assaulted day and night. I'm not trying to make excuses, but people reading this will find that very difficult to understand unless you've been through something similar yourself.

Today, I need to remind myself that these people no longer control my life or matter and I no longer need to look to them for approval or love.

I was literally broken when I signed that letter, and no more than an approval junkie desperate for crumbs of affection. It was as if my father was the only one that mattered in our relationship. And I would have done anything for him. That man caused so much suffering to me, but it took me a long time to come to that realisation. Had I known then what I know now, I would have told him to shove that letter up his arse and give it to my mother. There's a terrible shortage of toilet paper in that house.

MAMMY'S PET

The mere sight of him made me feel sick. This bloated monster had no redeeming features, and even as a teenager, he looked like an over-sized rat and smelled just as bad. He was a filthy animal. If he had a bath and you pulled the plug, you'd have to shove the water down the plug-hole with a stick.

He was about five feet six, wore bulky clothes to disguise his over-sized frame and had a Conor McGregor style swagger that made you want to kick him up the arse. He dressed mostly in black and wore what looked like a long leather coat. Underneath he had these scruffy pants covered in food stains and a pair of hand-me-down shoes from St Vincent De Paul.

He never hung around girls of his own age and was always following us kids about. We knew nothing about predators in those days, so we were easy targets.

Every chance he got, he'd try to put his hand down your knickers. But a lot of us shrugged that off as if it was normal. It used to happen so often we treated it like any other form of touching, but none of us knew how to stop that happening. I hated when he did that, and I froze every time. I would get such a fright I couldn't move. And I didn't dare tell him to stop. He would pinch me really hard if I did, and that hurt so much. At night-time, some of us would wake up in shock to find him molesting us while we were asleep. He would sit on the floor between the two beds, shoving his fingers into us under the sheets, and it was terrifying. One time another sister woke up and screamed at him, "what the fuck are you doing?" and he'd say, "I'm just looking for something?" and scurry off. That happened a lot, but whenever it happened to me, I instinctively froze. I couldn't even speak. Sometimes, I wasn't sure if I was awake or asleep, but I always knew when I was being assaulted. Being touched in your sleep is such a terrifying experience, it's almost impossible to describe. Whenever I was molested, it made no difference if I was asleep or awake. He did it to me anyway because he knew I would never fight back.

I could never sleep properly at night waiting for him to turn up, and that's still the case to this day. I often wake up at night with a jolt, expecting to see his disgusting face drooling over me.

He was every child's worst nightmare. A loathsome creature; a real-life monster who attacked children in their most vulnerable state. And whenever I hear parents telling their kids there's no such thing as monsters, I think of him every time.

Nobody liked him, except for mammy. She doted on him, but in a weird way. He slobbered all over her like he was her pet dog and to look at the two of them, you'd never think they were mother and son. It was disgusting when I think about it too much and some of the rumours that flew around about the pair of them were best left unsaid.

I could never understand why she held him in such high regard, and especially after she found out what he was doing to us? That changed nothing between them and if anything, it only made their relationship stronger.

She continued to call him her number one, long after he was made to leave the house by social workers. I used to call him her number two because they both blocked the toilet in our house.

The fridge was where you found him most of the time and he always had his big fat head stuck in there.

The smell was the first thing to hit you when you opened the fridge door. It was that rotten meat smell.

For a while, I was convinced our fridge had something living in it. It wouldn't have surprised me to come down some morning to find it making breakfast. That fridge was the perfect breeding ground for all types of bacteria. You could have won a war with some of the things hiding in the back. It never got cleaned and was constantly making strange noises. If you put a pint of milk in our fridge, half of it would be gone by the time you got back and other things like mammy's grub just disappeared altogether.

"Where's me fookin' ham, you thievin' fookers?" she'd roar at the top of her voice, and someone would shout back, "the fridge ate it!"

That made her go mental. She always blamed us for any missing food, but nobody else was allowed near that fridge except her or the monster.

The monster would eat a dead cat off the side of the road if mammy didn't get to it first. They would ate each other come to think of it but I don't want to go there!

There wasn't a lot you could do to make our mammy like you, and after a while, you stopped trying. But to a child, the more a parent rejected you, the harder you tried.

Thinking back, it was a complete waste of time, but that's how it was. Whenever anything was wrong, it was always our fault, and you never dared question that because you'd get the head kicked off you if you did. Mammy and daddy always knew best, but in hindsight, they knew feck all.

To my mind, there was obviously something wrong with me, because why else would the monster be allowed to do what he was doing?

Both my parents knew what was going on but turned a blind eye to it, and that was the hardest part of it all. At first I didn't want to believe that was true, because that's not how it was in the books I read. Parents didn't allow monsters to hurt their children, but it was different in our house. We got hurt all the time, and they knew about that. They knew everything that was going on. Some of my underwear used to be blood stained, but they never asked me anything about that? It wasn't like we were menstruating because we were too young for periods, but I used to wonder what would it take for them to notice we were being hurt? How many bad things did they need to see before they made the monster stop? They never asked him any questions. And that was another reason why I remained silent.

"Only bad things happen to bad people," my aunt Breda used to say, so I figured I was one of those really bad kids. But I wasn't sure what I was supposed to have done to make me so bad? I couldn't understand what I did to deserve all this torture I had to suffer each day? I had never stolen anything or hurt anyone? I always did my lessons in school and never missed any homework. At the very worst I was a bit cheeky now and then but no more than any other child my age.

I didn't want to be touched the way the monster was touching me and I wanted him to stop hurting me. But I didn't know how to make him stop. So I thought about running away. But where do I go? I was too small and had no money. Do all kids suffer like this, I used to say to my dolly? But she never answered me. She was only a doll, and she was kinda broken, too.

KILLER WASH

Our bedroom was like a prison cell with visiting hours between 7 and 8 o'clock. On a hot summer's day, it was unbearable. The heat left you bathed in sweat and with no window to open; it was almost impossible to breathe.

Winter was the complete opposite. The stale air in our room reeked of body odour, because most of us hadn't washed in days. The heat from our bodies would steam up the windows, and there was a rush to draw pictures on the glass in the morning before it was time to leave for school.

The bath was nearly always full of dirty washing and even though we had a washing machine, my mother refused to have anything to do with it.

Months earlier, she had been loading it up when she put her hand on some part of the machine and got a shock. Mammy hit the floor like a sack of spuds twitching like a mad thing. I was next door when I heard a scream and a thump and when I looked around the corner; I thought she was dead.

"Mammy, are you alright?" I said not too loudly in case she woke up, but she never said a word.

I shouted up the stairs for my sister and told her to come down real quick.

"Gzuz, what happened to mammy?" she said, looking at the hair standing up on her head.

"She's after getting a shock and I think she's dead!"

"Oh!" says Michelle; "is that what happens to your hair when you get electrificated?"

"No, dizzy, you mean electrocuted?"

"Yeah, whatever!"

"Look, you go get Uncle Sean from up the road, he'll know what to do?" I said.

"Alright so, will I call into aunt Breda and tell her mammy's dead and to make a few sandwiches for the funeral?"

"No, go straight to Uncle Sean's and don't mind asking anyone, anything."

"Why can't I ask her?"

"Coz you can't!"

"Why can't I ask her to make sandwiches?"

"Because now's not the time for fook sakes!"

"But, I'm hungry, and she'd give me loads and there'll

be ice cream and everything. Do you remember when Uncle Frank died, that was mighty grub altogether?"

"Will you shut your face you? Hurry up, and g'wan and get Uncle Sean, will you!"

As my sister hurried out the door, I looked back again at mammy splayed out on the kitchen floor and I didn't know what to make of her.

She was lying on top of a big heap of dirty washing and still hadn't budged. I couldn't tell if she was dead or unconscious but I needed a school blouse for tomorrow and mammy was lying on top of it.

I'd never touched a dead body before, but I'm sure she wouldn't have minded if I shoved her out of the way.

I figured if I got a brush under her, I could lift her up just enough to grab the blouse and wash it in the sink.

But I remember someone saying something about not touching anyone with electricity going through them.

You might get a belt yourself, so I decided best leave well alone. Anyway, if she was dead, we probably wouldn't have to go to school tomorrow, and that'd be that problem solved.

Apart from that, there were loads of other thoughts flying through my head, but most of them were fairly good ones in fairness.

As my sister said, there'd be loads of grub at the funeral, so that was something to look forward to. There was never much to look forward to in our house. Daddy might miss having somebody to go to the pub with, but give him a day or two and he'd be grand. The beatings would be over too, and I figured most of the neighbours couldn't be arsed if she was dead. They hated mammy up and down the street and Mrs Hannigan in particular. She'd be delighted. She said mammy was on her back so often she could get a job modelling linoleum.

Mrs Hannigan and mammy hated each other, and when she realised we were telling on her, she threatened to murder us all in our sleep if we ever said another word about her again.

But could you imagine getting killed stone dead by a washing machine? What were the chances?

All the neighbours would want to know what make it was. Mammy wasn't the only one they wanted to get rid of, but there was no fear of the monster doing any washing.

When Uncle Sean came strolling through the front door with my sister stuffing her face full of crisps, mammy was almost awake. They weren't in any great rush and looked half disappointed she was still alive. Nobody really wished her 'dead, dead,' but it was the quietest we'd ever seen her in years.

When mammy sat up, the hair was all standing up on the top of her head and she looked like she'd seen the Holy Ghost. She was as white as a sheet.

Mammy had to have come as close to dying as anyone but the Nuns used to say, 'never worry about that because there's always someone waiting for you in Heaven when you do.'

Mammy looked fairly dead to me, but I couldn't think of anyone who might be waiting for her? Maybe that's why they sent her back?

I'll tell you why, said aunt Breda. "She'd terrorise the Angels. You couldn't let her in anywhere."

I wanted to know if mammy got to meet the Blessed Virgin Mary while she was half dead and if she did, did she get to see what Heaven was like and all that?

She probably got told to feck off at the front gate, but she wouldn't have fared much better in Hell, either. The Divil would have her barred within minutes.

"What happened to you, Stella?" said Uncle Sean, trying not to laugh. He had on that half worried look on his face, but I think he was toying with the idea of plugging

73

her back in.

"Holymudderojazuz," said mammy, looking up at him, while wrestling with her top set of dentures.

"Did you got a bad oul' dose?" says Sean, thinking she had just floated back up the toilet bowl.

"I did, is fookin,' right!"

"Are you alright?"

"Do I look all fookin' right?" she says, examining her false teeth, to see if any were melted.

"Did you get a bit of a knock?" said Uncle Sean..

"Yeah, off that fookin' thing!" said mammy, shoving her teeth back in.

"What thing?"

"That fookin' thing, there!" she says, gesturing impatiently at the washing machine.

"Don't touch that for now?" says Uncle Sean, raising a palm up in front of her, "I need to knock off the electricity."

"I've no intention of fookin' touchin' nottin'. That's after givin' me a horrid fookin' belt," says mammy, staring at the washing machine like it was possessed.

"You look a bit shook alright, did ya slip or what?" says Uncle Sean, looking down at all the water on the floor.

"No, I didn't slip, I got electratuted!" That thing put me

on the broad of me back?"

"And it didn't even buy you a drink?" says Uncle Sean.

"What are ya fookin' on about?" says mammy.

Mammy spent a lot of time on her back, as everyone knew, but Uncle Sean wasn't too sure if she had pissed or shit herself, and neither were we?

"Do you think you broke anything?" said Uncle Sean, looking at me and smiling.

"I think I broke a bone in me hole," says mammy.

"Do you want me to call you an ambulance?" he said.

"You can call me what you fookin' like. I'm not movin!"

"Well, stay where you are, then so?" said Sean.

"I will in me hole, for what?" says mammy.

"In case ya broke anything?" says Sean.

"Sure, what about me? T'wouldn't be the first time! D'ya not know how many times I've fallen on me arse in that fookin' street?" says she.

"Jazuz, you're right about that, Stella. I think we need to get ya a pair o' drawers to match the pavement?"

I roared laughing, the minute he said that.

"Don't you be laughing at me, ya little cunt?" says mammy.

Uncle Sean started tip-toeing around mammy like she had shit herself, but it was hard to tell. He wasn't too sure if the water he was standing in was belonging to the washing machine or her. But he wasn't taking any chances. Mammy was a dirty oul' trout at the best of times, and she could piss on you at the drop of a hat.

"Holy jazuz, this house is in an awful bloody state," said Uncle Sean, muttering under his breath.

There was always a smell of shit in our house and as mammy slowly pulled herself off the floor, she suddenly let out one of the most humongous farts I've ever heard in my entire life.

At first, we didn't know what the sound was, and then it hit the back wall of the kitchen and blew open the back door. It was like someone had shoved a football up the arse of an elephant and tied off the other end with a rope. This was an ungodly explosion, and even the birds started coughing.

"Oh-mudder-o-sweet-jazuz-what-in-the-love-o-fuck-was-that?" says Uncle Sean, making a beeline for the backdoor.

I couldn't breathe, I was buckled from laughing and the tears were now streaming down my legs.

Seconds earlier, Sean was trying to figure out where the smell was coming from, but now he knew. He was out the backdoor like a shot. We all were!

Mammy's farts were a terror. The back of her skirt was
all wet, but only the bomb squad would dare to check.
"Do you need a hand in there, Stella?" says Sean, hol-
lerin' from outside the backdoor, hoping she'd say no.
The thought of cleaning up mammy's mess was the last
thing on his mind, but getting farted on was the worst.
She was known for it. She let off several at a horse with
the fright one day, after it wandered in the back door of
our house. The poor creatur' wasn't the better of it. Out
to fook, it thought it would never get. You could see the
legs going out from underneath it as it struggled to
breathe.

We heard a big loud 'prrrfffttt' and everyone thought it
was the horse at first, until we realised it was mammy.
No horse's fart could ever smell that bad. They had
grass farts. Mammy's would strip the paint off a wall.
Every time she got nervous or worked up, she would
fart. It was an awful affliction and daddy used to give
out shite about it, but that only made her worse. She'd
be going around the house like a deflated balloon while
he was having his stew and the stink would sicken you
altogether. She'd be minging.

Then she'd lose the rag and throw something and let off
another banger. I don't know which was worse; getting

kicked in the head or smelling one of mammy's farts? Daddy used to say nobody ever wanted to sit beside mammy in the pub. She'd stink them out of it, and that wasn't a word of a lie. The thought of getting locked into the bathroom after mammy was a fate worse than death. Nobody went in there for ages afterwards. Not even the flies. They knew better. It was like a crime scene. Someone locked the cat in the toilet after mammy and it started screeching its head off and nearly drowned itself in the bath trying to escape.

Whatever came out of mammy wasn't natural and what-ever she ate was even worse.

Whenever she and daddy came home from the pub, it sounded like she was about to give birth. She was so full of drink she used to walk home holding her head back in case she spilt any.

Sometimes she'd bend over, grab a hold of the railings at the front of the gate, and let rip at both ends. It was an awful sight and all the dogs in the street would start barking. The sound of her throwing up was rotten.

It was like someone tearing a sheet in half. I didn't think it was possible to vomit and fart at the same time, but she could do both and talk at the same time.

As we all stood around in the kitchen watching mammy

pull herself together, I had a swollen bottom lip from biting on it so hard.

Uncles Sean's face looked like he had been sucking on a Lemon and that set me off again. It was too much. I needed to pee again real bad, and I was cross-eyed with the laughter.

I had never laughed so hard in all my life and I kept leaving and coming back in case I missed anything. From what I could see, mammy looked like she needed to be bleached and Uncle Sean's nose was so high in the air, if he cried, the tears would run down his back.

That was the funniest thing ever, looking at him going around staring at the ceiling. He could see me fixing to burst out of the corner of his eye and frowned while smiling and pulling a finger up to his lips.

Mammy was now up on her hands and knees looking like a new-born calf while Uncle Sean looked for a mop to clean up the mess. They say you piss yourself before you die but this was a right Tsunami altogether.

"Stay where you are there, now, Stella, till we make you a nice cup'o'tea.

"Are you sure you don't want an ambulance?" he said, pinching the end of his nose.

"Fook dat!" says mammy, "And what are you holding

your fookin' nose for, did I shit meself or what?" she said, struggling to regain her balance.

Uncle Sean, didn't reply.

"The curse-o'-jayzuz on that thing," she said as she tried to stand up, 'prrrffftt,' "I think I'm after 'prrftttt,' shittin' meself, alright, 'prfffffftt,' pifftt, pifft, would one of yee fookers' ever 'prrrffftt,' give me a fookin' hand?" 'prrrfffttttttttt....'

"Eeewwww!" said my sister somewhere in the background.

"I knew that fookin' thing was going to be the death of me one of the days," says mammy.

"I think you're going to be the death of us all yourself, if you don't stop farting," said Sean, under his breath.

"Speak up, I can't fookin' hear' you?" says mammy.

"I said, I think you better shit.. sorry, sit down," says Uncle Sean, trying to figure out which was the more lethal, mammy's arse or the loose plug?

"I better, is fookin' right! There's smoke coming out me ears. I'm after gettin' a horrid roastin," says mammy, as she made a lunge for the nearest wall.

"One minute I'm standin' there, next minute, I'm on the flat of me back covered in shit! I wouldn't be as bad, if I landed abroad in the fookin' fire!"

Uncle Sean stuck his wrist in his mouth to try and stop himself from laughing. Whatever was coming out of mammy's ears was nothing compared to the other end. I think if mammy had actually caught fire there wouldn't have been as much of a stink. There might have been a bit of an explosion, but sure the house needed re-decorating.

Loose electric wiring would put the fear of God in you, but Uncle Sean was more worried about a gas leak, and mammy was the source.

Daddy had the washing machine fixed in no time, but it didn't make a whit of a difference.

The damage was done. Mammy had herself convinced daddy was fixing to kill her.

"Ya stupid thick cunt," was the first words out of her mouth when he arrived in the door, later that evening.

"What's the fookin' matter with you now?" he said.

"That washing machine in there is after nearly killin' me stone dead! And me teeth are all loose in me head," she said looking for sympathy and getting none.

"What's wrong with it?" says daddy.

"Who wired the fookin' thing? Michael, fookin,' Mouse?" mammy roared back at him.

"I'll take a look at it, after the dinner," says daddy heading towards the oven. "Who turned the lights off?"

"Sean did! And you may leave them fookin' off or we'll all be roasted in our beds."

"There's nothing wrong with the electrics in this house, it's probably just a loose wire."

"Well you're wastin' your fookin' time if you have it in mind to fix it," she says. "I'm not usin' dat thing, never no more!"

"That's a dangerous fookin' yoke. Look at the cut of me? I look like something the cat dragged in. And me new dress from St Vincent De Paul, all covered in piss and shite."

"Jazuz, I didn't notice much of a difference, in fairness? What did ya do to your hair," says daddy.

"What d'ya mean, what did I do to me fookin' hair?"

"Is that the new look, or what? it's all stood up on your head? You look like a mad pieball," says daddy trying his hardest not to laugh. Mammy hated being laughed at. She'd go pure ape on anyone who laughed at her and tear the place apart. She'd be the type the council would put the poles closer together for, so they could get her off the streets quicker.

"That fookin' machine did that, ya, cunt, ya!" said mammy.

"Jasus, I might grab a hold of that yoke meself, one of these nights?" he laughed.

"I haven't a fookin' clue what you're on about. I had the heart put crossways on me and only for the Holy-Mary-Mother-of-God, had mercy on me soul, I'd be burnt to a crisp."

"Speaking of which, is me dinner still hot?" says daddy.

"It should be; it's been in the fookin' fire for the last two hours,' said mammy.

"Ah for the love o'jazuzz, did you let the stew get burnt?"

"Fook you and your stew. I nearly got stewed meself and the whole fookin' house burnt down around me ears, and all you're worried about is your gut!" roared mammy.

Daddy ignored her. It was a wise decision.

She was getting herself worked up into another lather, and you got no good out of her when she started talking like that.

But from that day on, mammy vowed never to go near another washing machine again and she kept her promise. That demon contraption had nearly killed her, and if we knew then what we know now, we probably would have bought two of them.

BIGGEST DUMP

Everywhere you looked there was filth. Children's clothes were strewn all over the place, and the only way to really sanitise our house was to set it on fire.

The white lace curtains had stopped being lace years ago. All the lovely patterns were congealed from kids wiping their noses and hands on them.

The house was so damp, you'd torpedo the place quicker than demolish it. It was the type of damp that crawls in under your sheets and sits on the end of your bed like a frozen lake. Along the alcoves, black mould crept menacingly along the tops of the walls, while dog-eared wallpaper hung down in places where the spiders starved to death. Their delicate webs seemed to be the only thing stopping the whole house from falling apart, but even the flies had disappeared.

During the winter months, we were always frozen. Most of the time there were never any sheets, and only for the warmth from each other, we'd have perished in our sleep. We had one big hairy wool blanket between us which itched at your skin and was a haven for bed bugs. If the rest of the house didn't get you, the blanket would. There were more things living in our room than in Dublin Zoo and not half as ravenous. We were covered in bites and welts, and looked like we had the measles. This happened so often we almost knew which bed mites had bitten us. Some of us were so thin there was only room for 3 or 4 spots.

I shared a tiny single bed with my sister Helen and it was a struggle to get to sleep. She often had nightmares and would regularly wet the bed. The mattress became terribly smelly. If anyone asked which end of the bed did I prefer? It was always the 'shallow end.'

A few feet away, there was another single bed where my other sisters slept, top and bottom. Little things got on their nerves. They'd be pulling the heads off each other over the stupidest of things, but it 'wasn't as if they licked it off the ground,' as we say. I never fully understood what that meant until years later. You didn't dare lick anything off the ground in our house. You'd be dead within 5 minutes. The mice needed stilts to go across our floor and at 8 o'clock, we'd wait for the tide to go out so we could all go back upstairs.

Next door was mammy and daddy's room. That was an

awful sight. The wallpaper in their room was stained a dark green puke and the pattern on it had long since faded. The carpet was covered in all sorts. You'd need a blow torch and sulphuric acid to get it clean.

You couldn't hoover it. The bag would explode in seconds and refuse to turn back on. Mammy used to talk to something in that room whenever daddy wasn't at home. We didn't know if it was the wall or the floor. There were more things living in her bed than all the houses along our road.

Their double-bed was one of those old wire sprung frames from the 40s that could trap a small foot if it got stuck down the side.

Up top, was an old thin horsehair mattress that you didn't dare jump on. If you did, you were taking your life in your hands. You'd be afraid of waking something up or getting offended. Things used to scurry upstairs from the fridge and hide in there for days on end. Nobody ever knew if it was the mice, but none of us was about to find out. There were huge dark stains all over it, but I think if you whistled loudly, you could take it off around the fields for a walk. Sometimes daddy would put the mattress outside during the summer months to air it, but we think it was just for a change of scenery.

Uncle Sean said, "if you left that on its own long enough, it'd be gone, but it wouldn't be stolen, I can tell you that now? The cut of it," he'd say with disgust. "You wouldn't put a donkey on it! You could plant spuds on that mattress and she wouldn't even notice." Even the pillows were dodgy. They were darkened a deep yellow ochre from tobacco stains and vomit.

On the other side of the room, there was a single bed with a cot for the youngest before they'd be moved into our room. That'd be about an hour after mammy had brought the baby home.

The room next to our parents, was called the box-room. That was where the monster slept. He didn't have to travel very far to get to us. His room was always untidy, and it smelled of nicotine and socks.

Downstairs, the smell was not as bad, but got worse during the hotter months.

The carpet on the stairs was covered in filth and hadn't seen a hoover since the place was built. If you stamped on it hard enough, you'd start a dust cloud that would pollute the entire house. Where it had worn too thin in places, you'd catch a toe and trip up if you weren't too careful. Sometimes I used to wonder if the stairs was tripping us up on purpose. I remember sitting on it with my knees propped up against my chin, hoping that nothing would crawl out and bite me. There were things living everywhere in that house but they only came out at night.

If a neighbour came by to visit, my sister and I would sit on the stairs trying to listen in on the conversation just for something to do. No visitor ever got a word in. We had a small TV, but the picture was fuzzy and someone kept bending the aerial. The fact that it was plugged in, meant it was the only thing–apart from the couch–that mammy didn't throw at us.

Anything that wasn't nailed down or bolted to the wall she'd sling at you, and God help you if you didn't move out of the way quick enough.

In the middle of our bedroom, there was an old fireplace which daddy had blocked off because of all the mice. I remember him and the monster catching some alive and taking them out the back and cutting their heads off in front of us. I was horrified they would do such a thing. I was hoping they might keep their promise and let them go in the field, but they never did.

The monster thought this was hilarious, and I was so upset. It was the most upsetting thing imaginable.

They were only baby mice, but that didn't matter to him.
On the other side of the room, there was a big brown
wardrobe full of clothes with loads of rubbish inside. I
never liked that wardrobe. I used to think the bogeyman
lived in there and I always kept the door firmly shut.
Dirty and clean linen were all mixed up together and
some other stuff was thrown up on top.

Dolls and teddy's that had been handed down over the
years littered the room, along with whatever else was littered around the place. We never had dolls for very long
because the small ones would pull the heads and legs off
them.

The light bulbs were taken out of our room and the
windows were always sealed shut leaving the room full
of stale air.

The street lamp on the far side of the road used to
shine into our back bedroom and the light from that
was all you had if you wanted to read a book or a
comic. You had to strain your eyes really hard to see,
but it was all there was. We had to go to bed early at
about 6 or 7 o'clock before mammy and daddy went to
the pub, but reading a book always helped me sleep a bit
better and it took my mind off the pain. The pain was
always waiting around the corner, and so was he.

One summer evening, at the back of our house, I went out the door to see if my friend Mary was about. We had been feeding this pony, and we wanted to take her up for a run round the field. The gate was open, because the farmer had been cutting the hay, so we ran off up the gap with the pony running alongside us thinking we were like a pair of race-horse owners. At the time we thought we were great, but had the pony decided to do its own thing that would be the end of that. We had no saddle or rope to control it, but in those days, ponies went wherever they wanted to go.

The field we were in was huge and sometimes the grass got so tall you'd have to jump up and down to see where you were. But to us, this was mighty craic and just rolling around the grass and flattening it into circles was the best thing ever.

Next minute, Mary froze as if she'd seen a ghost and I didn't know what she was staring at for a second. As I slowly turned around, I saw him silhouetted against the brow of the hill as he slowly made his way down the slope towards where we were playing.

I could feel my heart thumping out of my chest and Mary immediately said to me, 'come on Lorraine, I think we better be going?"

"I can't, Mary. You go ahead; I'll follow you in a minute," I said. "No, please, come now," she said. "I want you to come home with me now, Lorraine, please?" she said pleading with me as tears welled up in her eyes. She squeezed my hand more tightly than usual and it was at that moment I realised she knew.

"I'll be fine, honest. I'll see you tomorrow," I said, giving her a quick hug.

Mary looked at me as I was about to burst into tears, but I pushed her shoulder softly down the slope.

"Mary, go!" I said. "Please? You can't stay here."

And then we looked at each other. As our eyes met, we didn't need to say another word. We were both sworn to silence, but neither of us dared to speak. Mary looked at me as the tears rolled gently down her beautiful face, and I remember saying to myself. "No Mary, noooo, not you too? Please say it isn't true?"

But suddenly the monster spoke and we both jumped. I don't know what he said, but Mary ran away as fast as she could and I looked back to make sure she was safe in the distance. Then I waited.

TWO APOSTLES

Most nights we went to bed early and if she wasn't in the pub, mammy would send the monster off to the shops to buy some Tayto crisps and a bar of chocolate, but never anything for us.

He was told if there was someone visiting to leave them on the stairs so mammy could get them when they were gone. Sometimes a neighbour would overstay her welcome and of course, kids being kids, we'd tip-toe back down the stairs, snatch the treats and share them quickly amongst ourselves. We knew there'd be killings, but we didn't give a shite and anyway, we were really hungry. When the neighbour left, you could hear the roars of mammy all the way down the street.

"Which one of yee little thievin cunts took me Tayto and bar off the fookin' stairs," she'd scream at the top of her voice.

"Tell me now! I'm only going to ask yee once, for the third time. Who took them, now don't make me come up them stairs?"

Naturally, none of us would own up. Then she'd fly up the stairs in a fit, lean over the top of us, demanding to smell our breath. The pillows muffled most of the screams, but it was worth the hiding coz we all loved chocolate.

Ripping mammy off became a regular past-time in our house and on Wednesday nights we used to go down to the local convent to say the holy rosary.

After praying our faces off for an hour, Sister Assumpta would bring us down to the kitchen to give us something nice to bring home.

Fresh buns were the best treat ever, and having them straight out of the oven was even nicer.

"Now girls, I've put a half brown bread and a bit of dripping in the bag for your mammy as well."

My sister and I looked at each other with devilish grins, and apart from thanks, we didn't need to say another word. Those twelve small buns were gone. We both knew they'd never make it out the convent door, never mind the front gate. We devoured them quicker than you could say, 'mammy's going to kill us!'

After a minute or two of gorging ourselves, we were stuffed. But we knew it was only a matter of time before we got caught. And in fairness, we didn't give a shite. Fresh buns go all over the place and it's very hard to hide the evidence, but that wasn't what caught us.

This particular night, we made the mistake of shoving the empty wrapper they were kept in back in the bag. When we got in the front door, the first question mammy asked was; "well, how did yee get on tonight?"

"Sarah sang a song; Helen said a Novena and two decades of the Rosemary and I....?"

Mammy wasn't interested in none of that. She only wanted to know what was in the bag. She stuck her hand out, snatched it out of my hand, and quickly pulled out the dripping and brown bread.

The dripping was thrown to one side and the brown bread got a squeeze to see if it was fresh. Then the wrapper followed next and she eyed that suspiciously.

'Shit!' I said to myself, as I looked at my sister nibbling away at the bottom of her lip. We forgot to get rid of that!

"And in this bag, was what?" she said, as she looked at each of us in turn. There was a long pregnant pause....

"Well... speak up, yee two little fookers; answer me?"

"No, that was ehmm, that was all, that was all she gave us," I said.

"Was it now," said mammy staring at all the crumbs in my hair.

"And, what was in this?" pointing a nicotine-stained

finger at the bottom of the bag while holding it out-stretched like you'd hold up a dead mouse by the tail.

I stared at the bag stone-faced and said, "ehmm... that was ehmm, that was a bun!"

"Oh, it was a bun was it! Just the 'one' bun you say?" said mammy, knowing full well I was lying through the crumbs in my teeth.

"Well, yeah," I said.

"Did yez enjoy them buns, did, yez?" says mammy, scenting blood.

"It was only the one bun," I said.

"The Sister gave it to us, and she said we could share it." It was all I could think of to say, but I knew where this was going, and I wasn't a great liar, to be honest.

"So there was only 'one' bun in that bag, was there now, well we'll see about that?" said mammy.

I looked at the floor and said nothing and glanced across at my sister, hoping she would keep her mouth shut.

This was touch and go, and we seemed to have got away with it for now, but when mammy was on the hunt, things could go from zero to shit, in 60 seconds.

The following Wednesday, we were back at the Convent, and mammy turned up outside the door unannounced.

Just as we were about to head home, with another hot bag full of buns. Her timing was impeccable.

"Well, helloooo Sister Assumpta," mammy said grabbing our two wrists in a motherly fashion, and cutting-off any chance of escape. "I thought I'd come in to pick up the girls. I was just was passing by," she said.

'You lying fookin' trout,' I said to myself. 'There could be the two of us lying in the middle of the road face-down with a cardboard sign in big red letters with our names on it and mammy wouldn't so much as look at us,' I felt like saying.

"Ah, very good," said Sister Assumpta.

"And while I have you, we want to thank you for the 'bun' and the brown bread and the dripping," said mammy.

This was the same dripping that the cat was choking on earlier and the brown bread nobody saw a slice of.

"Ah, you're very welcome," said Sister Assumpta. "And there's another twelve buns in that bag as well, same as last time."

"Oh, thank you so much, you're so kind. Twelve you say?" said mammy.

"Oh, yes, twelve, we always give twelve. One for each of the glorious Apostles," she said looking at mammy and blessing herself furiously.

My sister and I stared at each other and our expressions said it all. We were fucked!

"Is that how many there were?" said mammy as she slowly glared at us in turn with daggers in her eyes.

"Well, that's grand then so sister Assumpta. I think eleven of the Apostles must have fallen out of the bag last time but I'd better take these two Apostles home and have a word," said mammy.

"Oh, dearie me, I hope I didn't get anyone into trouble?" said the Sister, not realising she had just sentenced us to a slow, agonising death.

"No, no, not all," says mammy giggling hysterically, "you know what some girls can be like?"

"Oh, I do, I do, I do, well God bless you all and safe home," she said, as we got dragged off to the slaughter-house.

"You thieving pair of fookin' cunts!" she hissed, as mammy closed the gate of the Convent with a loud metal bang behind her.

"I'll break your fookin' necks, the pair of yee. Yee ate all them fookin' buns, yee selfish pair of cunts."

"We were hungry!" I screamed in protest, as mammy lashed out with the back of her hand at each of us in turn.

"I'll redden your buns when I get yee two fookers home. You'll get fook all to eat tonight, I can tell you that now."

Nothing new about that, I said to myself. We got feck all most nights. But from that day on we never saw another bun again. Mammy insisted that the bag be double tied, in between beating us half to death, and if there was so much as a crumb on either of our heads we'd be strangled to death.

Later on, we planned to sneak down the stairs and do a raid on those buns. But there were always strange noises coming from the kitchen. Maybe the fridge was on the move again, or a monster was on the prowl; you could never really tell? Staying hungry felt safer. We were in no fit state for another beating.

MAMMY DEAREST

My father gave strict instructions that if I was to turn up at the church on the day of his funeral, they were to push his coffin back out the door and leave him there till I was gone. Well, I laughed when I heard this. 'Don't flatter yourself, you dirty looking eejit,' I said to myself. 'I might just turn up halfway through the ceremony just to spite you.'

But honest to God, where would you hear the likes of it? You couldn't be right in the head with stupidity like that? Could you imagine the look on everyone's faces? And the whole lot of them pushing on the coffin with the priest lashing holy water at them as they go back out the door?

I have to confess, though, the thought of my father being fecked back out into the car park had me in stitches. What if I was to go out for a fag break halfway through the ceremony? And what happens if I have two fags instead of one? "They'd be better off leaving him outside," my husband said. "Sure, you'd be fit for the coffin yourself, with all that draggin' in and out? And anyway, if the ceremony is of a Sunday, the binmen in Birr come around Mondays so they can pick him up.

You can't have rubbish like that lying around the
church. And they can borrow my van if they don't.
I'll get rid of him down the bog. And why not keep the
coffin for that other lunatic who needs jail? He won't be
long needing it himself. The boys in Mountjoy will sort
him out with a few belts in the mouth," he says.
Mammy you couldn't bury in a coffin and if you did,
you could never reuse it. The wood would be pure
rotten within a week and the place covered in rats. She'd
pollute the whole cemetery. You'd have to cremate the
woman and tell everyone to stand well back. You'd need
about three weeks to put out the fire. She's 100% pure
alcohol and shaped like a jar of Bovril, so the coffin
would have to be bombproof. And if they did cremate
her, I swear to God, you couldn't put her in an urn. The
thing would explode and you'd never get the smell out
of the house. You'd be better off sprinkling her ashes
all over the front room. I guarantee you, nobody would
notice the difference. She'd love that. She creates most
of the dust in the kip as it is, and her favourite line
about me is; "that one would walk all over ya!" and she's
right; I'd love to! So you know where to put her? On the
floor, where I spent most of my childhood.
Anytime I went down the street with her she'd let a roar

at you; 'Get out of the fookin' way of this person or that and watch where you're going?'

'Sorry about that now,' she'd say ever so politely to whoever was passing by and then further on down the street we'd meet another neighbour and she'd look at me and not mammy and say; "Lorraine, how are you today?"

Mammy would be raging whenever that happened.

"Oh, don't bother talking to that one, that one's very bold," she'd say.

"Ahh, now don't be like that, Stella," the neighbour would say, looking at me with tears welling up in my eyes.

"Oh, she's a bad one, that one!" and you'd be left standing there mortified, not knowing where to look.

The neighbour could see I was getting upset, and she'd pat me on the head to reassure me that I was okay.

I overheard one neighbour in a shop saying about mammy, "I don't know what to make of her?"

I felt like saying, 'a rug!' but I didn't want to sound cheeky.

Another neighbour would say, "she looks like something the cat ate and threw up! Would she not look after herself?"

My mother would talk so much shite she'd get a cramp in her face. She went on with pure rubbish, and it was all about her. Where she came from, they used to sell Father's day cards in packs of five.

You'd know people were mad to get away from her. They had things to do; but she had nothing!

After I left the house to move into a flat in the town, people used to ask me how were we getting on and I'd say, "she came around the other day, but we managed to sedate her again after a brief struggle," and they laughed.

One night, my sister whispered to me, there was a prowler downstairs in the kitchen, and she told daddy? He asked her, "what was he doing?"

She said, "he was eating something out of a pot mammy was cooking earlier, and daddy said to leave him where he is?"

"Did he not call the Guards?" I said.

"No," said my sister. "Daddy said, there was no point, he'd be dead by the morning, and we could bury him out the back."

Daddy distanced himself from us all, not because he disliked children necessarily, but because he seemed to have more important things to do. Every time he made an appearance, we were all over him. All eyes in the room were on him. Mammy would have a long list of things for him to do because she was too lazy to do them herself. Someone else would hush them into silence in case she overheard, but the unspoken message was always the same. This was a man we were all supposed to worship and obey, but it certainly wasn't for his parenting skills? Daddy wasn't a father in the protective sense of the word. He had relinquished that role long ago. Somebody talked about how we should have been grateful, but that means nothing to a five-year-old girl who just wants a hug after being raped a few hours earlier. Harsh as it sounds, he knew that was going on under his roof, and for reasons best known to himself, he chose to ignore that along with the violence from mammy.

Daddy did most things around the house, including the cooking. On those rare occasions when she did try to cook, mammy would send us down to the fish stall and ask for scraps. You wouldn't feed them to a cat. She'd fry that up and give it to us on a dirty plate. It was disgusting and full of bones. You were taking your life in your hands if you ate it and the same again if you didn't.

She'd let a roar at you, "ate that up to fook! Yee un-grateful little cunts! If yee don't, I'll belt the fookin' head off yee!"

You'd be pulling bones out of your throat every few seconds and the image of a fish's head staring back at you on the plate always stuck with me to this day. Mammy loved fish, eyeballs and all, and she'd eat one raw as quick as look at you.

One day she walked out of the room while we were sitting watching TV, and when she came back, most of her chips were gone.

"Oi, c'mere, now, ya cunt, ya," she'd roar at daddy in the kitchen. "Did you cook that fish proper?"

"What are you fookin' talking about now?" says daddy, sticking his head around the corner.

"That fooker's after atin' all me chips?" says she.

"Stella, don't be talkin' shite. It did no such thing?"

"I'm not telling a word of a lie. All me chips are fookin' gone?"

"Bring me back that fish, and I'll cook it some more?" says daddy rolling his eyes to heaven.

"No," says mammy, poking at the fish with her fork to see if it was still alive. "You'll make it too dry."

We were great little actors, you'd never think to look at

us. We just sat there, poker-faced, looking at the TV while trying not to laugh and swallow at the same time. You didn't dare chew. You could only swallow. We were like ventriloquists.

We could demolish a whole packet of biscuits without moving our lips. If she made us open our mouths, we were fooked. She'd choke the head off you and make you spit everything out into the fire.

Other times, she'd send you down to the local bakery to get a loaf of bread, and if the colour wasn't to her liking, she'd send you back to get a replacement. It had to be black on top, because that's how she liked it; burnt to a crisp like herself.

And that was her bread and nobody else's. None of us would get a slice, and especially if it was fresh. There might be some leftover the following day, but by that stage, it was gone all stale.

She'd sit there in front of us with her cup-of-tea, quarter pound of ham with fresh bread and stuff her ugly face as if there was nobody else in the house except her.

It didn't matter that all the children were hungry. Mammy shared nothing, and more often than not, we went to bed on an empty stomach.

One day they caught my sister stealing food from a local shop. I stood outside looking in at her through the window, and didn't know what to say or do. I was so embarrassed.

Next minute she appeared in the window waving a packet of biscuits like a mad thing. She was acting like she owned the place, but I knew she hadn't a bob to her name.

Brazen as you like, she'd bounce out the door like a spring lamb with two ice-pops and a packet of bars, but that's about as far as she got. Two hands suddenly grabbed us from behind by the scruff of the necks.

It was the owner of the shop, and she looked none too pleased.

"Now girls, I don't think you've paid for what you have there?" she said, politely but firmly.

"Don't be lookin' at me," I said. "I never took nothing from no shop?" almost in tears.

"No, not you, this one!" she said, pointing at my sister, who looked up sheepishly and said, "I'll get mammy to pay you tomorrow?"

"No, sorry, it doesn't work like that. I'd like you to hand them back now, please, if you don't mind?"

My sister did mind. She shoved everything behind her

back, and the cheeky head on her told me, she was fixing to do a runner.

Don't you dare, I said to her, glaring at her as hard as I could. She was worse than a Terrier holding onto a rat, and for a second or two it looked like a stand-off.

If she bolted, we'd never be able to show our faces in the town again and it was bad enough she had already been caught.

I stared my sister out of it as hard as I could, but there was no shifting her. The woman was still stood there, becoming increasingly impatient, with her hand outstretched.

"Now, young lady, are you going to hand those back, or not? Or do I have to call your mother?"

That worked. Seconds later, we were stood there empty-handed, wondering what to do next.

"Don't you be saying nothin' to mammy, or she'll bate the head off, of me!"

"Are you mad in the head or what?" I said.

But we both knew it was only a matter of time before Godzilla found out.

Mammy would normally go shopping herself of a Thursday and that's when the shit would hit the fan.

The idea that two of her two girls were caught thieving

didn't bother her in the slightest. It was the getting caught bit she was mad about. Mammy would rob the eyes out of your head. If ten cents fell out of her purse, it'd hit her on the head. She was so mean, if she went to a fortune teller, she'd only have her finger read.

"What the fook, were you two fooker's doin' the other day?" she roared at me first, and then back at my sister shaking in the chair.

I tried to explain that I was outside the shop when my sister was doing all the robbing, but I might as well have been talking to the wall. Everything was all my fault because I was the eldest of the two.

"You should have had more fookin' sense!" she said, hitting me a slap.

"Ma, it wasn't Lorraine's fault," said my sister, as mammy threw another slap in my direction. "Shut to fook up you! She should've had more fookin' sense!" she said.

Get up them stairs the pair of yee, you're gettin' no grub tonight for your sins, yee pair of little cunts!"

Three hours later, I was back downstairs, lying on the filthy floor. I could feel his hands pulling up my flimsy nightdress and dragging at my underwear.

I immediately tried to focus on the sound of the Grandfather clock on the wall to block out what was about to happen.

It wasn't a big one like you see in those fancy houses, but I got a lot of comfort from that clock. It seemed to move with the beat of each thrust.

The first sting of pain was like an electric shock followed by another and then another that seemed to go on forever.

I squeezed my eyes tightly shut, only because that seemed to help. Anything to block out the pain.

At 8-years-old I was only a slip of a thing and this was too much to cope with.

Every muscle of my tiny body was fighting against the force of him. I could barely breathe. I felt like I was in the grip of a gigantic vice where no part of me was able to move.

I wanted to die there and then, but before I did; I had to pray to the Holy Mary, Mother of God, and ask for forgiveness. Because what was happening was all my fault and this was my punishment for being a bad girl and taking mammy's chips.

I prayed I would never take anything ever again. If only she could just make this pain go away. I would be a really good girl from now on. But I don't think she heard me that night, or the night after that.

This was the prayer I'd say to our Lady every night and I still do to this day.

Hail Mary, Full of Grace, The Lord is with thee. Blessed art thou among women, and blessed is the fruit of thy womb, Jesus. Holy Mary, Mother of God, pray for us sinners now, and at the hour of our death.

Amen.

NO SANTA

Christmas day always brought back terrible memories for me, but one Christmas in particular stood out among all the rest.

I was only about 10 years old. We had two houses next to each other, and my father always left the Christmas presents in the house next door.

Mammy and daddy would go to the pub on Christmas Eve and after they arrived home, Santy would do his thing, meaning he would wrap all the presents up and have them ready for opening the following morning. For any child on Christmas morning, it was a time of great excitement and we'd hear them coming in from next door with the bags.

Daddy would call all of us downstairs and make us sit on the three-seater couch over in the corner of the front room. He would then reach into the bag and say to mammy with great drama, now I wonder who this is for?

My mother would then point a finger at whoever it was and there'd be a big scream and rush of excitement and paper shredding to find out what you got.

When everyone had collected their gift, I was left sitting there wondering why my name hadn't been called out? The younger ones had got books and dolls and stuff; small things they were delighted with, but I couldn't understand what was taking them so long to get to me? The anticipation was too much, and I couldn't wait any longer. I looked at the empty bag on the floor with a half expectant look on my face, thinking this was a game.

"What about me, daddy?" I said, whereupon he looked at me surprised and then back at mammy who was gathering up all the loose wrappers.

"Oh, sure you're too big now for presents, you don't believe in Santy any more!" said mammy, as she shoved the papers into the fire.

I stared back at her in disbelief, and then at daddy, hoping she was only joking, but she just turned around and walked out of the room without saying another word. Daddy shrugged his shoulders, held his hands up and

looked at me as if to say, it's nothing to do with me, I
only live here.

I couldn't believe this was happening. I was stunned!
He didn't even try to soften the blow. I burst into floods
of tears immediately and ran straight up to my room.
My aunt Breda dropped by some time later and she
wanted to know what Santy had brought us all.

I was still sobbing at this stage and when she saw me at
the top of the stairs with the big red-rimmed eyes, she
immediately wanted to know what was wrong?

I said to her in between big heaving sobs, "I got nothing
from Santy for Christmas," and burst into tears again.
She threw mammy and daddy a filthy look, took me by
the hand and brought me up to her house to meet her
cousin Joe, who had recently returned from Australia.

I was too embarrassed to look at him because I was in a
terrible state, but the damage was done. The shock of
being left off Santy's Christmas list was all I could think
about. I still believed in him at the time and all this
kindness was only making me more upset.

Joe gave me money and Aunt Breda gave me a big hug
and something to eat, but I knew they were only doing
their best to make up for what had happened in the
house that morning.

I looked at my aunt Breda crying, "is it true what mammy, said?" I sobbed.

"Is what true, little pet?"

"That Santy is not real, and that's why he never brought me anything?"

"No, darling, that's not the reason," she said, as the tears rolled down her face and she hugged me tightly once more.

Much as she tried to fix things, Christmas was never the same again after that.

What should have been a day of celebration and joy turned out to be one of the saddest days of my life? I have never known rejection like it or since, and it seemed unimaginably cruel for my parents to do what they did. I am now married with children of my own, but thank God none of my children will ever know how that felt. For them, Christmas is a great time of celebration, but for me, it left indelible scars that I am still struggling to erase.

TREE ON THE HILL

On the 31st of October 2017, I made the tough decision to return to the scene of the crime. The small town in Offaly where it all began had changed a lot since the 80s. Housing estates and supermarkets had replaced large green fields that were once teeming with rabbits, and it was sad to see they were all gone.

Everywhere I looked, something had changed, but the memories of the past remained the same.

I was feeling anxious as I climbed over an old steel gate. It looked like it hadn't been opened in over forty years, and it felt a bit like my thoughts at that moment.

The fields behind our house were a natural playground for all the kids growing up on our road, but for me, they harboured terrible memories. This was the hunting ground of a serial predator and the big tree at the top of the hill was where he abused his victims.

For a moment or two, a sense of panic gripped me. I was unsure of my surroundings and I looked around the field, anxiously retracing my steps, trying to figure out where it had got to. It had to be around here somewhere? And then I saw it; lying there at the brow of the hill, or what was left of it?

That magnificent tree that had once stood so proud had been chopped down and looked nothing like I remembered it. What remained was a mound of twisted limbs and branches piled up on top of each other and it bore no resemblance to the big, majestic tree from my childhood memory. If anything, it looked a lot like how I felt at that moment. From where it once stood, you could see the whole town in every direction and for a monster, it offered the perfect vantage point. But that beautiful old Scots Pine was never meant to provide that type of cover. Now, like me, this glorious piece of nature lay shattered on top of that hillside. Its torn and broken limbs spoke to me from where it lay. As I looked around at what was left of its magnificence, all the horrible memories suddenly came flooding back.

'Come over here,' I could hear him say in a gruff voice. I jumped whenever he spoke, but always did as I was told.

'Lie down!' he barked.

I hesitated, but only for a second. He would hit me if I did. I thought about screaming out, but kids screamed all the time around here and nobody paid much attention. Maybe bad things like this were happening to them too, but how could I know that? Did they have secrets like mine? Mammy always used to tell everyone how bad I was, so this was all part of my punishment, and I dismissed the thought that this was wrong. But I still wanted to ask other girls, did their brothers do what mine did to me?

But I didn't dare ask in case he found out. Asking questions like that might only make the monster angry.

And anyway, this was meant to be kept a secret.

I couldn't understand what was going on. And even though it was a secret, I still needed to make sense of this terrible nightmare.

As he unzipped his black trousers, I braced myself for what was about to happen next.

Staring at the Buttercups helped. If I looked at those little yellow flowers long enough, I didn't have to think about what was happening.

I could feel his hands pulling at my underwear as I lay there motionless, waiting for it to be all over.

I looked at those Buttercups waving in the breeze, and tried to imagine what it must be like to be so small. Maybe they felt like I felt at that moment. I wanted to cry, but I was never allowed.

I could smell his rancid breath on my face and I tried to hold my breath so I wouldn't have to smell anything. I hated the smell of him.

The grass held the dandelions aloft as they swayed in the gentle breeze. I loved blowing those fluffy dandelion puffs, but suddenly I could barely breathe.

The weight of him on top of my small frame was too much, and I started to feel faint.

Ever so often, I'd catch a glimpse of his face and it frightened me. He had this contorted expression, and I couldn't understand any of what was happening, or why he was making those faces.

He swore me to secrecy once more, and then it was over as quickly as it began.

I desperately wanted to tell someone; but who? Who could I trust? Who would understand? Who would explain what this monster was doing to me, and why must it be kept a secret?

It was a horrible secret, and I didn't want to keep it any more. Mammy was the last person I could talk to about anything like this.

Even if I could, I didn't think she would believe anything bad about her precious son; and as it turned out, I was right and she still doesn't believe it. Mammy would tell me to shut my mouth like she always did.

If my sisters did anything wrong it was always my fault so this must be my fault too.

So, I kept my silence not just out of fear of what might happen if I told anyone, but because deep down I knew this was all my fault. I deserved what was happening and that's what I had been told. If you can't trust your own mammy and daddy, who can you trust?

So, I resolved in my mind to put up with all the bad things and that's how it remained for the next thirty years.

I was 43 years old when I experienced a major health scare after two lumps appeared on my chest following a routine examination. A battery of tests followed and thankfully they turned out to be benign, but it was a scary time and I had convinced myself that all the years of bottling things up had finally caught up with me. I never allowed myself to think about the things that had happened to me as a child. There was always something else to do, and cleaning was my biggest distraction.

I could clean a house from top-to-bottom and then start all over again if somebody so much as left a fingerprint. I drove myself nuts but a family friend explained to me that all this cleaning was probably a displacement activity.

I didn't know what that meant at the time and to be honest, I didn't really care to ask; I just wanted to clean everything. It brought me some sense of relief. And it didn't help that I was brought up in an absolute kip.

I wasn't so obsessed that I didn't allow any muck in the house at all but cleaning was a form of therapy for me. The physical act of cleaning was more important than the finished result. I knew I could never erase all the horrible memories of my past, but cleaning something solid was the next best thing. I didn't think of it that way at the time, but that's how it was explained to me and it made a lot of sense.

Depression was the other thing I had wrapped around me like a heavy blanket, and towards the end of 2016, I was as low as I had ever been in my life.

It felt like I was being punished in the present for my

sins of the past, and once again I blamed myself for everything.

I was becoming increasingly irritable, and the slightest thing set me off. My children knew something of my past, but not the details. I felt I couldn't really tell them what had really happened without upsetting them or causing distress.

Even my husband didn't know all the details. For years after we married, I still couldn't bring myself to talk about what had happened in that house. Even now, stuff is still coming back that I thought I had forgotten. But the pressure of keeping everything a secret for so long was taking its toll.

And then something remarkable happened. A new neighbour moved in beside us and suddenly everything changed.

Our lives were turned upside down. In a dramatic twist, the dark side of the Irish justice system that had failed me so miserably the first time was about to be exposed. Some of the people whose job it was to protect me as a child turned out to be my worst enemy, and this man was about to become their worst nightmare.

CHARITY SHOPS

We were so poor in our house, all the mice went to live in the church. All our clothes were hand-me-downs from neighbours or friends and Heaven knows we didn't have many of those. One neighbour used to say, "Lady Luck will smile on you some day," but by the time she smiles on me, she'll have no teeth left? I felt like saying.

When the house went on fire, none of us were too bothered. Whatever nerves we had left were well and truly gone. A screaming child in any confined space can be difficult at the best of times, but when you don't know where it's coming from, it can be really annoying. While a lot of screaming went on in our house, there are few things that can turn the whole house mental quicker than the sound of screeching. It's the type of high-pitched sound you associate with nails being dragged across a chalkboard, and there's nothing more nerve jangling.

The wardrobe in our room had caught fire after one of my sisters inside was playing with matches. Next minute, the whole room went up, including the curtain next to

the window. And that's when Matilda started squealing.
Getting up, and taking a look, never occurred to us.
Our house went on fire a lot. The house was always full
of smoke and especially whenever dinner was ready.
But when the screaming got worse, and smoke started
billowing down the stairs, I figured something was up,
but nobody bothered to move.
That's when part of the front room ceiling collapsed.
It just fell down in front of us with a big bang.
We all looked at the dust cloud, and then at each other,
like it was the most normal thing ever.
One of my sisters went back to watching the telly.
"Is that dust going to be all over the dinner?" she said.
"It might improve the taste?" I said.
"I couldn't give no fooks, I'm starving!"
"Did mammy's cooking cause that?"
"Looks like it, yeah!"
"Well, it's after putting a big poxy hole in the ceiling."
"Did mammy blow the lid off the big pot again?"
"How am I supposed to know, don't ask me?"
"The pot hit the roof last time too an' all?"
"Daddy did too, an' he's going to be raging?"
"I don't think it was mammy's cooking?"
"I reckon, it was!"

"Sure, how do you know?"

"Sure where else could the smoke be comin' from?"

"I dunno, go ask mammy?"

"Who's doin' all the screaming?"

"Matilda is!"

"Matilda, shut to fook up, will ya?" someone shouted up the stairs. "I'm tryin' to hear the Telly!"

"The room is on fire!" Matilda shouted back.

"Well, put it out?" they said.

"I can't!"

"Why not?"

"It's too big, and the curtains are all on fire..."

"Did ya try stamping on it," I said back.

"How is I supposed to stamp on the curtains, ya big eejit?"

"Noooo, ya retard, the floor?"

"Yeah, I did, but now there's a big hole in it. But it's nice and warm and there're loads of pretty sparks and stuff coming off the wall?"

Turned out it was the warmest our room had been in ages, but that didn't last very long. There wasn't much left to burn, apart from a few beds and all of us.

Next minute I saw a load of mice running down the stairs and I knew that probably meant trouble.

126

"Maaaaaa?" I shouted into the kitchen. "The mice are after running down the stairs?"

"What d'you want me to do, put a fookin' plate out for them? What are you fookin' on about?" I'm tryin' to cook in here and this cooker is actin' the cunt!"

"Ma, there's a big hole in the ceiling?"

"Don't be fookin' annoying me. Leave it to your father to fix, when he gets home?"

"But maaaa?"

"Will ya ever shut your mouth, you, there're holes all over this house and you need to shut yours or I'll shut it for ya!"

"I don't think daddy can fix this hole, maaaa?"

"Oh, for the love of jazuz, show me this hole now?" says mammy storming into the front room impatiently with a wooden spoon in hand ready to strike.

"Oh, sweet Holy Mary Mother of God!" said mammy, looking up at the big hole in the ceiling and dropping the spoon with the fright.

"The house is comin' down around our ears. Get out ta' fook the lot of yee!"

Nobody moved.

"I think the house is on fire?" I said.

"Wouldn't fookin' surprise me! There's always sumthin'

on fire in this house?"

"Will yee get out to fook!" mammy said again.

"For what, ma?"

"Whaddya' mean for what? Can't ya see the hole in the fookin' ceiling and the place on fire.....?"

"But it's only a small fire, and Matilda is still up there, and she's still roarin,' so she's not dead, and if she's not dead, why do we have to leave?"

"Matilda! Come down those fookin' stairs this minute."

"For why?" Matilda protested.

"Don't answer me back. Come down those stairs, now!"

"But maaa, it's nice and warm up here?"

"I'll give ya warm. Yer arse'll be on fire if ya don't come down those fookin' stairs, this second?"

Matilda was fascinated by the flames and would have stood there all night looking at that piss fuelled room go up in smoke; we all would!

That room symbolised so much evil for us all. What went on in there could never be burned from our memories. By rights, they should have burnt the whole house down years ago, along with someone else.

The monster was gone off somewhere, and more's the pity. You'd be tempted to lock his door from the outside and tell the Fire Brigade to go away and come back later on. As things turned out, a neighbour had already called them, and they arrived real quick.

When two fire engines pulled up outside the house with sirens blazing, nobody was in any rush to leave.

Anyways, it was too cold outside, and we were only dressed in our nighties.

When one of the Fire Brigade men burst through the front door, the sight that greeted him was surreal.

All the kids were still sitting around watching the Telly while a fire was raging above their heads. There was no sign of any mammy. You wouldn't see the like on the movies. One of my younger sisters turned to the other and asked, "who's that lad with the helmet and stuff?"

"I dunno, I think he works with daddy?" she said.

"He looks fierce scary with that big axe and all?"

But before we could say another word, we were all swept up off the floor and whisked outside by all these lads in fire helmets. It was really cool, and we were loving all the attention. Somebody warned the men not to go near the big pot in the kitchen.

Mammy's cooking was more lethal than any big fire and that could burn the whole street down. Nobody knew what was in that kitchen and nobody dared ask?

Mammy used to cook things that would follow her

home and other stuff that had gone off well before we were even born. She had a secret stash hidden away, and some of it used to escape and start a fight with things in the fridge. There could be anything going into that pot, but only a few of us ate it. We weren't allowed ask questions, and maybe it was just as well. Mammy couldn't read the labels on anything and the sniff test was all she used. But sure you couldn't smell anything in our house? Everything smelled rotten!

The only way you could test anything raw in our house, was to leave it alone for half an hour, or cook it before it escaped.

I was half hoping the kitchen would catch fire as well, but it didn't take them long to put everything out.

All the neighbours were out in the street watching this carry-on and mammy was lapping up the attention.

"Oh, Holy Mary Mother and Joseph, sure, isn't it a mercy we got out by the skin of our teeth?" she'd say. "I know, Stella, I know, aren't yee blessed? Yee could have all been killed in your beds?"

'The lying trout,' I said to myself. Sure mammy went straight back into the kitchen to check on the dinner never mind the skin on her teeth? Only for the Fire lads, we'd have all been sitting there sucking air through a

hole in the wall wondering what all the fuss was about?
There was smoke in our house almost every night. This
was nothing. One room going on fire or the roof falling
down would probably improve the look of the place.
At least all the shite would be gone off the walls and we
could start to breathe through our noses again?
Mammy spent ages chatting to the neighbours about the
fire. There were loads of people dropping by to see how
we were doing and asking did we need anything?
But the minute they left, she'd bad mouth everyone
behind their backs and cut them asunder.
"That one doesn't give a fook!" says mammy.
"She wouldn't piss on ya if ya were on fire. She's only in
here for a nose. And that other wan' from up the way is
only wantin' to see if there's a few bob floating about?
And did ya see that other yoke, with the big worried
head on her? Sure, she's mad with the drink and the
other one living next door riding every fella in the street.
The fookin' cheek of them coming down here, and
stickin' their noses into my business? Ya think they
never saw a bit of smoke in their lives?
And me sitting here with the heavy load on me mind
and your father off playing darts while all of his
children are being burnt out into the street; where da

fook is he?"

"Sure, you couldn't be puttin' up with any of fookin' dat? There's not wan' decent neighbour in this street dat gives a flyin' fook about me and that house?"

"I swear to fook, if I walked up that street tomorrow morning with me head on fire, none of them fooker's would put themselves out? Ya could be dyin' roarin' on the flat of your back with a crucifix stuck up your arse and not wan' of them would pay a blind bit of notice or say a prayer for ya? Am I right, or am I mad in the head?" says mammy.

When it came to mammy arguing, she was both, but the majority of people in our street were decent working-class people who looked after us in so many ways and genuinely cared. They brought us down food and blankets and everything and told us we could stay in their houses till ours was fixed.

I think mammy just disliked people in general, including the fact that they had cleaner houses than ours.

The Samaritans would hang up on her. She was totally illiterate and had a big chip on her shoulder about that. Mammy used to go up to Dublin on the bus and get our clothes from the charity shops.

We had no toilet roll in the house. Newspaper had to

do. But with so many other children in the house that was in short supply, too.

Mammy and daddy were always fighting about something, and nine times out of ten, it was mammy who started the row but daddy would always give in.

I would often sit and watch the two of them snarling at each other like cats and dogs. They showed no affection at all. Not so much as a smile, and I used to wonder what my father saw in her? There must have been a desperate shortage of women when he was growing up. Mammy was foul-mouthed and mean spirited and a horrible person inside and out. She let her straggly hair grow long but seldom washed it or tried to keep herself nice.

She looked like a wicked witch, or the Banshee from Darby O'Gill in the Little People. She was irritable, and the atmosphere in the house was always horrible whenever she was around. If she was angry—which was most of the time—she'd hit you with whatever came to hand. That could be a poker, a shovel or whatever. And the more you screamed, the more it seemed to spur her on. She only stopped hitting you when she was worn out. And the awful thing about her temper was that when it was over, she would carry on as if nothing had happened.

It was as if she took some sort of sadistic satisfaction from dishing out pain. I would run up to my room and cry my eyes out, but it made no difference. She never tried to make things better.

Next day I would go to school covered in bruises but nobody took any notice. I was dirty too.

We had no shower to wash ourselves. We had a bath but it was always full of dirty washing and daddy used to put his bike in there so there was no room to get clean. In school, we would get bullied by the kids about the smell off us. They called us the 'dirty O'Driscoll's' and they were right. We were! So we said nothing. It was safer that way. There was no point in going home and telling our parents we were being bullied because they obviously didn't care.

Around Easter and Christmas time, they'd have recitals in our school where all the parents would be invited to come along and watch their children on stage.

Mammy and daddy never came. I was so embarrassed and jealous of the other girls in my class. I always felt different from them. They had pretty, shiny hair. Snow white ankle socks and clean clothes whereas I looked like something the cat dragged in. My clothes stank. My

hair was knotted from never having been brushed properly, and I just didn't fit in.

I had one friend, Mary, who would always stick up for
me. She lived on my road and we were friends from
when I was very young. Mary would often bring down
clothes and shoes to our house, and it was not like she
came from a well-off family, either. She was just a kind-
hearted person with a big heart and always had a bright
smile.

Mammy didn't like her, but that came as no surprise.
She didn't like anyone I was friends with.

When the school bell rang to tell us it was time to go
home, my heart always sank. Most of the other children
would be falling over themselves to get out the school
door. I never felt that way. I dreaded the thought of
going home. The prospect of having to endure several
more hours of abuse felt like I was heading home to my
own funeral and, in a way, I was. I was slowly dying inside, but nobody could see.

MONSTER CALLING

I was frozen to the pillow 'Lorraine, come down here now!' he bellowed up the stairs. Maybe I could pretend not to hear him and he'd call someone else.

Mammy and daddy were barely out the door 2 minutes when he called out my name.

'Lorraine?' he'd shout out again, banging the bottom of the step with his fist.

I could feel my whole body tensing up. The sound of his voice made my blood run cold. If only I could find somewhere to hide; but where? There was nowhere safe to hide in that house.

The wardrobe was the best place, but that was too scary. What if I got locked in and couldn't get out?

They nailed the windows in our bedroom shut and even if they were open, the drop to the yard below was too great. I was way too small and skinny to fight back and the monster compared to me was nearly double my age and size.

As I shuffled off my end of the bed, I looked back at my sisters for a moment, but they were all pretending to be asleep. It was only 7 O'clock. I knew they were wide awake, but nobody wanted to catch my gaze.

Whenever the monster called, nobody dared be awake in case they were next. Even if we were wide awake, there was nothing to do but pretend. There was nothing any of us could do or say to make this better. There was nobody to utter a kind word. All I needed was somebody to say 'it'll be okay and you'll get through this' but nobody ever said those words.

I got called most nights, but sometimes my other sisters got called instead of me.

I could only hope that it would be over quickly and go back to bed, but nobody asked where I was going or what I was doing because they knew. We all knew. Asking questions only made it real.

As I made my way downstairs, my legs shook uncontrollably. I was petrified and could barely cover the last few steps without holding on to something tight.

As I hesitated for a few seconds, he shouted again, "Lorraine, hurry up!" and I almost lost my grip with the fright.

Sometimes I prayed for this to be all a bad dream and that any second I would wake up somewhere safe in a place like Heaven. But it never happened, and the monster was always in the same place, in the middle of the room, in the middle of our house, half-naked, with his arms crossed like the Devil in heat.

Then he would pounce, and then I would scream as loud as I could, but only inside my head. He never heard a sound. That was always my secret.

School was the same. All the other children were around my age, but they all looked so neat and tidy compared to me. I used to see them chatting amongst themselves in huddled groups, and sometimes I wondered if they were talking about me. Did they somehow know what was happening, or could they see it on my face?

Mary, my best friend, used to come running up to me whenever she saw me in the playground on my own, and it always delighted me to see her.

'How are you?' she'd say with a big, sunny smile.

'Grand, and how are you?'

'Grand! What you up to?'

'Not much. How about you?'

'Did you watch Nancy Drew on the telly last night?'

'No, I missed that!' Unable to tell her why.

Much as I loved her, I could never talk about anything like that. It was much easier to change the subject and talk about something else. But little did I realise she was being molested, too. We were both victims of the same monster, and for all those years, she never said a word. I was distraught beyond belief when she told me what happened to her over thirty years later.

She said she didn't want to tell me in case I blamed myself, and she was right about that. I blamed myself for everything, and she knew that was in my nature.

Had she never met me, I thought, that would have never happened, but my writer again came to my rescue.

"Nobody in that street where you lived was safe," he said. "And I think it's important to mention, none of us are ever responsible for another person's decision to abuse another child. The fact that he abused your friend was an outrage, but I think he would have found a way to get to her, with or without your friendship."

Mary never minded me not talking. She always managed to pick up on how I was feeling, and that's what I loved about her. She could talk about anything and best of all, she seemed afraid of nothing. She was a right little soldier and always rallied to my defence whenever the bullies started on me.

The second someone opened their mouth, she'd be all over them like a rash.

"You leave her alone, or I'll pull the head off of ya!"

Mary might scream. And they'd run off with the fright. I was too terrified to stand up for myself like that, but Mary never backed down from a fight.

She was much stronger than the other kids in our class, but you'd never think to look at her. She was really tall and whenever she got into a fight; it was all over in a few seconds.

She was a few years older than me and could probably tell a big part of me was in an emotional sling.

I never needed to tell her what was actually happening to me at home. I think she knew instinctively something was wrong or too painful to touch.

Some girls, even at that age, can pick up on those things real quick and that was what made her such a good friend.

She had seen how mammy behaved whenever she picked us up from school and that also helped a lot.

I didn't need to explain mammy lashing out for no reason because Mary had seen it happen with her own eyes.

But you didn't talk about your parents in those days, no matter how badly they behaved. Nobody did!

The Nuns also used to remind us, if you've nothing good to say about someone, don't say it all but I'm not

so sure if that meant ignoring people who raped us?
I don't know what they might have said about that, but I
know you're reading this Mary and you've no idea how
much your friendship meant to me. You obviously knew
instinctively something was wrong because it was happening to us both and it's what bonded us. But I am so,
so, sorry, you had to suffer that evil too. Nobody never
knew because nobody never said, but I want to thank
you for always being there for me when I needed you
most. I love and miss you to bits and I'll talk to you very
soon.

x

Love Lorraine

DIRTY BLACK MAT

The monster never brushed its teeth and his body odour was like that of some dirty mongrel that spent all day swimming in a rat-infested canal. I hated the smell of him. It was the type of putrid smell that makes you want to scrub your skin till it bleeds and if it wasn't for the fact that I had to go to school next day, I'd have torn myself to shreds.

'Lie down!' he'd say in a gruff voice.

I hesitated for a second, but always did as he asked. If I didn't move quick enough, he'd get angry and pinch my arms.

As I lay down on the large black carpet in the middle of the living room, the smell off the rug hit me like a slap in the face. They had spilt everything you could think of on that toxic pile and I'm surprised it didn't follow me up the stairs whenever I got off it.

Underneath that again was a sheet of brown-coloured linoleum with bullet sized cigarette holes everywhere.

Lying there, trying not to heave, I would have given anything for a bottle of bleach.

The monster by now had unzipped himself and was

down on his knees. As he flopped down on top of me, his sudden weight forced the air out of my lungs like I had run into a wall. I felt dizzy. The shock of this foul-smelling whale landing on top of my tiny frame made me feel faint. I couldn't lose consciousness. Being awake was bad enough, but fainting was even worse.

Whatever he was going to do next, I just needed to get it over and done with. My senses were overwhelmed. The smell of him, the smell of the floor, and what he was doing was too much. I needed to focus on something else. The TV was turned on with the volume down. Somewhere in the background was the sound of the kettle boiling on top of the range.

A picture of our Lady hung next to an old grandfather clock that made a gong at the top of the hour.

I preferred to listen to that instead of him. The shiny pendulum seemed to move at the same speed as me, but then it would move faster.

My whole body was being slammed back and forth like a rag doll, and I thought my back was about to break.

I wanted to scream at him to stop, but I was afraid. Every thrust sent shockwaves of pain up through my spine that made my head want to explode. I couldn't breathe. This was horrible torture and I had no way of making it stop. I could hear his breathing get louder, then he would grip the carpet hard on either side of my head and start to quicken the pace.

Did he not realise how much this was hurting me? Can he not see the agony on my face? How can someone do this to a child? My eyes welled up with tears, but I hadn't enough air left to cry. The pain in my tummy hurt so bad, but I prayed and prayed it would stop.

I didn't know what he was doing or why he was doing it, and I didn't care anymore. All I knew was that I hated how it made me feel. I just wanted to go back to the safety of my room and not wakeup.

MAMMY'S DAY OUT

I never much liked Saturday's because that was mammy's day-out. She always picked one of us to accompany her, in case she got shit-faced, and today was my turn.

The routine was always the same. We would make our way out onto the Roscrea road and mammy would start this circus act in an effort to get a lift.

I was too young to know what she was at, but to me, she looked ridiculous. Mammy had the leg swinging out in front of her, hanging off the pavement and hitching up the skirt.

"What are you doing that for?" I asked.

"Just you fookin' watch!" says mammy.

I couldn't understand what she was at? Mammy was nothing to look at, and if that tree-trunk leg of hers was supposed to get us a lift, we'd be waiting all day.

She had a face like a bulldog chewing on a wasp and she was giving all the cars these mad looks as they drove by, but nobody was stopping.

As she hopped comically from one foot to the next, to me, she just looked like someone who wanted to pee. She kept bouncing up and down like one of those pole dancers, and I couldn't see the sense of it.

The cars seemed to speed up when they saw her, not slow down. And anyway, Nuns used to warn us about thumbing a lift, but I don't think mammy had anything to fear. She was more worried a sex maniac might jump out from behind a bush and ignore her.

After about 15 minutes of these antics, a car pulled up ahead of us and mammy runs up, pulls open the passenger door to ask where he's going?

"I'm heading to Cork," said the driver, will that do you?"

"I couldn't give a fook where you're going once it's in that direction?" says mammy as she hopped into the passenger seat and I hopped in the back.

Two minutes later, I could see the regret written all over his face. Mammy wore this cheap perfume that smelled like air-freshener, but the next minute she farted as she shifted in the seat. A few seconds later, his nose started twitching like a mad thing as he frantically opened his window on the driver's side.

"Jazuz, it's a bit hot outside today, and we could do with a bit of fresh air," he said.

He was about the same age as daddy, and his car smelled really clean, but mammy soon put an end to that.

No sooner had he the window open, mammy was off like a hare to try and distract from the fart. The conversation went nowhere. I could see the look on the man's face. He was trying to figure out which was worse, the fart or mammy's perfume?

I was mortified. All the colour had drained from the poor man's cheeks, and he looked like he was about to throw up.

'If you can hold your breath for the next 2 minutes, it'll pass,' I felt like saying, but I think he had gone deaf.

"So where are you from yourself?" says mammy, not waiting for an answer. Prrrrftttt.....

"I'm from back down that road where you picked us up and I'm going down to visit me sister. Her husband is not there anymore because he's fierce with the drink and my mother's cousin lives just over the cross next to my other cousin, twice removed..."

I could never understand that twice removed business, mammy always went on about when talking about her relatives. They were twice removed from what? An asylum; a grave?

"Is that right?" said the man, looking at her like he'd just picked up a dead sheep off the side of the road.

At that stage, I thought we were going to crash.

"Oh, that is right, is right, she's not an O'Driscoll mind, and has notions, but she's married to my father's brother and he's only from across the way but he suffers terrible with the nerves. But I hope it keeps fine for her now because there's talk about her and the local Priest because she's never out of the confession box, her younger sister is living in Dublin next to the barracks, do you know the barracks, sure how would you?

"Is that right," he said again, trying to get his breath back. The man looked traumatised. This was the closest thing you'd get to a tear gas attack, but less suffocating.

"Well, just up the road from where she used to live is all my father's family, they all come from there and one of the sisters is married to an O'Brien, she had a touch of the shingles last week and had to go to Dublin but she's over the worst of it now, but I think it's the change in the weather, it's been very damp lately and I think they're expecting a bit of rain this week, I had a touch of everything meself last week and sure I'm over the worst of it thank God, but sure you never know with this weather, it's all in the hands of the man upstairs and sure if we didn't have the bit of drink to look after us, sure where the fook would we be? I take the odd drop meself now and then but only for medicinal purposes, and what about yourself?"

Mammy held the record for the longest sentences ever, but since there's no off button, most people lose the will to live after about 10 minutes of listening to this shite.

I could see he was already starting to drive a bit faster, to get a bit of air going through the car, but mammy didn't notice. By now, all the windows were open and the man was half hanging out the window.

When we got to the next town, he couldn't wait to get her out of the car. 10 more minutes of mammy talking and farting and he'd have driven us over the edge of a cliff. Mammy had that effect on people.

"Where can I drop the pair of yee off?" he asked.

"Oh, anywhere along here," says mammy. I'm meeting me sister in the hotel for lunch," she says, all law-dee-daw, like.

'You are in your arse!' I said to myself. Mammy was never in a hotel in her life. She was heading for the pub and the only person she was meeting was herself.

As she struggled to find the door handle, she was still spinning away like an electric drill.

I could see the driver heave a sigh of relief as he

pointed to where it was rather than reach across her. The smell off mammy would melt the head of you and he didn't want to get any closer. He couldn't wait to get rid of her and for a second I thought he was going to give her a shove as she opened the door. "Thanks very much now, God bless, safe journey, I hope I didn't talk too much because you know yourself you wouldn't know what to be talking about these days," she says, stepping out of the car and forgetting to close the door. Mammy never knew when to shut up, but he looked back at me hoping I'd close the door instead and gave me one of those 'relieved' smiles.

"Really sorry about all that," I whispered, as I shut mammy's door and gave him an awkward wave.

Mammy was still on the side of the road after he had driven off, and if I hadn't pointed at the big blank space, she would have continued yapping away.

She'd be better off in the back of a cattle truck and be in good company too. They don't come out with half as much shite and smell a whole lot better.

Two hours later, I'm sitting in some smoky pub watching oul' lads drink themselves sick and mammy screaming her head off. She was always flirting like a mad thing and got worse when she needed more drink.

Mammy could drink any man under the table and back up again, but I was mortified by this carry-on.
She'd be licking the face off them like a bitch in heat and I got fed up of looking at this after a few minutes.
There was never anything to do in that smelly pub, but nobody bothered to ask would I like a mineral?
I just sat there watching all these dirty looking eejits removing the colour from their pints.
All they seemed to do was go back and forth to the toilet and talk pure shite. I couldn't understand them?
One fella mammy was with eventually threw me some change to get rid of me. I rushed off out the door to the shop at the end of the street. I was starving and hadn't eaten all day, but I hadn't enough money to buy anything decent. I had enough for an ice-pop or a packet of crisps, but that was about it. I was still hungry a few minutes later.
After what seemed like ages, mammy fell out of the pub and into the nearest chipper to stuff her drunken face. If I got a chip from her bag, I was lucky, but that's about all I got. She never bothered to get me anything. She had to be one of the meanest fookers you could possibly meet, and that's not a word of a lie.
I probably got an extra chip that day, but that was only

because she dropped it. "You can have that," she'd say, and continue to eat the rest of her chips in front of you. I may as well have not been there.

Be grateful for small mercies my aunt Breda used to say, but as we made our way back onto the road again to thumb a lift, I felt nothing but contempt.

I hated the sight of my drunken mother staggering along the road with the smell of alcohol, fish, and fags trailing along behind her. I hated the fact that I had to sit in some smelly, smoky pub all day along with dirty oul' lads pulling and dragging out of me and covering me in spit when they spoke.

I hated that she was hanging out with other men and kissing the face off them in full view of everyone. What would daddy say if he knew about all that carry-on? I was mortified. People in the pub were looking and talking about her. They knew she was married.

Years later, I found out daddy said to my sister Helen, "once she comes home to me, that's all that matters." When we did get home later that day, I couldn't believe mammy and daddy were planning to head straight out to the pub again. That could only mean one thing.

DEADLY SWING

There was only a few days to go to my tenth birthday and it was a beautiful sunny day. Summer in June, where I grew up, could be glorious. Nearby, there was a small little playground that doubled up as a crèche for all the kids in the neighbourhood. This day, I was on one of the swings while someone from behind gave me a push.

As the swing went higher and higher, I screamed with delight, and then suddenly I saw him in the distance. Standing there at the edge of the wood like a Fox eyeing its prey. For a second, I hoped it wasn't him.

Maybe I mistook him for someone else, but as he beckoned me over, I could feel my throat tighten.

There was no mistaking that long black coat and white shirt. From a distance, he looked like an undertaker that had just crawled out from one of his own coffins.

Funnily enough, the 'undertaker' was what they used to call him on my road, but to me, he was just a monster. He was every little girl's worst nightmare and as I slowly brought the swing to a halt, I headed off in his direction and braced myself for what I knew was coming next.

153

None of the other kids paid any attention to where I was going and there was no parent around to ask for help.

There was no getting away from him. He had me in his grip. I had been trained like a circus monkey to do exactly what he wanted, when he wanted, and I hated how that made me feel.

I felt totally powerless in his presence. But I used to bargain with myself, if I just do as he says this one time maybe he'll leave me alone.

It was a forlorn hope, but as I made my way over to where he was waiting my legs started to tremble again. I wanted to run away, but I couldn't muster the courage. Something was driving me forward, and I never understood what that was?

Why am I letting this happen I used to say? Why don't I just scream out loud? The answers to those questions, of course, came much later, but as I lay down in the middle of that wood and looked at the sky above, I could see what looked like Angels in the clouds.

I wondered were they watching what was happening, and if they were, maybe they could tell someone?

DEAR MRS FLINT

I regularly visited an elderly neighbour of ours, Mrs Flint, and sometimes she'd send me down to the shops to run a few errands. The daily routine was much the same; I'd get home from school, change out of my uniform and get over to Mrs Flint's house as quickly as I could. The minute I was in the door, she always made a big fuss over me and dished out loads of hugs. I loved that about her. It didn't matter what mood I was in, Mrs Flint always had a good word to say, and had time for everyone.

Her shopping list never changed. Twenty No.6, twenty Woodbines; a carton of milk and £1 for my troubles, as she liked to call it.

£1 was a lot of pocket money in those days, but I never got to keep it. Mammy always took it off me, but I hadn't the heart to tell Mrs Flint in case she got upset.

We used to sit and chat for ages and I always felt safe in her company. Those visits meant so much to me, and she was like a proper mammy. The type of mammy I had always wanted but could never have, and that made me really sad when I thought about it.

Sometimes I took a bath in her house and it was such a treat. Our bathroom door had no lock, and it was full of bicycles and dirty washing that were always in the way. Even if you could get clean, the clothes you wore were never washed properly and stank of cigarette smoke or mildew. It was the type of smell you get when you leave dirty washing soaking for too long and it lingered under your nose for the whole day.

In the morning I used to lie in bed staring up at the ceiling, trying to process the pain from an attack the night before. I was always sore, and sometimes it was hard to walk. My sister was usually asleep beside me, and I could feel the warmth from her body as I waited for her to wake up. That was comforting, and I liked the closeness.

Morning time in our house was like a traffic jam. Everyone wanted the toilet all at the same time, and sometimes my little sisters couldn't wait. They'd go to the toilet wherever they stood and mammy would never bother to clean them or change a nappy. She always left it to us, but we never had any bleach or cleaning fluids, so we just had to make do with whatever we had which was water and a dirty old rag.

After a while, the smell became unbearable, and

especially during the summer months.

My Aunt Breda used to say, "why don't you potty train those kids?" and my mother would reply, "sure what harm is a little bit of piss going to do to them?"

Aunt Breda looked at her with total disgust. The whole house stank to high heaven, but it was nobody else's place to tell mammy what to do.

"She should mind her own fookin' business," she'd say. Mammy reared the children the way she saw fit and if the whole house smelled like a toilet, sure what harm? Daddy, on the other hand, did his best to keep things clean but as he was out working all day, so there was only so much he could do.

When he came home, he'd have to cook and clean while mammy lounged around the place watching TV.

The only time she got up off her lazy arse was when it came time to visit the pub.

Whenever she did do something for us, like visit the charity shop to pick up some clothes, it was all done be-grudgingly and nothing was ever the right fit.

Daddy fought with her constantly, but it was a waste of time. He wasn't able to cope with her explosive anger. She used to call him terrible names in front of us and used the foulest language imaginable.

'You're nothing but a lazy cunt!' was one of her favourites. 'How did I end up marrying a useless good for nothing fooker like you?' she used to say.

She was only talking about herself, of course, but it took me long enough to figure that one out.

'What are you fookin' staring at?' she'd scream at me or one of my sisters.

'I'll give yee something to fookin' stare at!' and a shoe or some other missile would come flying across the room.

Daddy never had much to say about that and wasn't much better when it came to violence.

He'd sometimes take his belt off his trousers and beat us black and blue.

One day mammy picked up a shovel and beat me around the head and body so hard I ended up staying in my aunt Breda's to recover. I remember I could barely move. Every part of me hurt from head-to-toe and the psychological trauma still lingers with me to this day. It was a terrible beating for any child to endure, and especially after being hit with a spade.

Had my aunt Breda, who saw what was happening, not intervened, mammy would have probably killed me. That's how lethal she was. You didn't have to do anything in particular. Just a look was enough to send her into a rage.

Mammy was a dangerous, sadistic psychopath, and woe betide anyone who looked at her sideways. If you tried to run away, she'd chase you up the stairs and drag you back down by the hair, head first. The more you screamed, the harder she hit. All you could do was curl up in a ball, cover your face and hope for the best.

"You little fookin' bitch," she would hiss. "I'll teach you to give me dirty fookin' looks," and she'd hit you a crushing blow to the side of the head that would send you flying. The pain was crippling and often times, I'd start to feel faint.

"D'ya hear me, you little cunt?" she'd say, in between blows and all of them as painful as the next.

"Look at me while I'm talking to you and stop your fookin' crying. I'll give you something to cry about!"

There was no getting away from that type of assault and I could feel my body beginning to shut down.

There were times I thought I was losing the battle but some small voice always told me to hang in there.

I had heard people talking about someone being beaten to death, but you don't realise how easily that can happen until you experience it yourself.

Blows to the head are so dangerous and a brain bleed is

the most common cause of death among children who have been seriously assaulted.

"Answer me, you little bitch?" she would scream, but all I could do was whimper. I wasn't able to absorb that type of violence. I was too small.

My mind could cope, but my body couldn't. As the tears streamed down my face and dripped onto my pale blue skirt, I felt utterly smashed from head-to-toe. The damp spots on my dress were growing larger by the second. I knew I had done nothing to deserve this, but my pleas for mercy always fell on deaf ears. Nothing I could say or do seemed to make her want to stop.

The thought occurred to me that maybe mammy was evil too, but I quickly dismissed it. How could there be that many monsters in the one house?

But despite what was happening, mammy was forever reminding me it was all my fault. If she was going to kill me, I prayed she would get it over with, and quickly. I just wanted the terrible pain to go away.

When the beating did eventually stop, it was through sheer exhaustion on her part.

She simply didn't have enough energy left to continue. At the time, I figured, I must be really bad to deserve all this to make her behave that way. And that might explain why the monster wanted to hurt me too.

I would often lie in bed after he had molested me, and think about what I had done earlier to make that happen. I couldn't make any distinction between what he was doing and what mammy was doing. Both were as bad and both involved a lot of pain.

But the monster had sworn me to secrecy. If I spoke to anyone about what was happening or to someone like aunt Breda, 'I'd be taken away from mammy and daddy,' he said. And as much as that terrified me at the time, thinking back years later, it might have been a blessing? Anywhere else had to have been better than that house. But for now, I was going to take whatever punishment came to me from those monsters and keep my mouth shut.

NEAR DROWNING

We were told not to come home till we heard the six bells ringing at the local Church. Mammy and daddy had gone somewhere for the day and we were on our school summer break. We didn't mind being left alone. We were having fun. I was the oldest amongst us at 10 and my younger sisters Martha and Helen were 8 and 9 years old.

The local river was fast-moving and deep during the winter months, but at that time of the year, it was safe enough to paddle in. We didn't have proper swimsuits, so we just played at the edge of the water in our underwear, throwing stones and splashing each other as children do.

None of us could swim and when it came time to go home, I couldn't find our younger sister Martha. She had obviously run back into the water when she heard the bells ringing and when I saw her, my heart nearly skipped a beat.

I could see her head bobbing up and down in the water as she desperately tried to break the surface for air. Her arms were flailing back and forth, trying to grab onto something.

I screamed at the top of my voice for help and ran to the edge of the water where she was floating, but it was way too deep and I couldn't swim. A feeling of panic and total helplessness gripped me.

My 13-year-old cousin who had been playing nearby heard me scream at the top of my lungs and rushed over to where I was standing. He saw the look of horror on my face as I frantically pointed at my sister slowly disappearing below the surface. I pleaded with him to go get her, but he didn't need to be told twice, and dived straight into the water. I felt my whole body freeze with terror as I saw him make a grab for the top of her hair just as she was about to go under again.

'Oh my God! Oh, please, please, God, let her be okay?' As he gathered little Martha up in his arms, she started to cough and splutter like she'd swallowed half the Brosna river.

That had to be a positive sign? At least she was still alive!

As my hero of the hour steadily made his way up the bank with my little sister shaking in his arms, we looked at each other in shock. The sense of relief we both felt at that moment was like nothing I had ever felt before. We continued to stare at Martha anxiously as we sat down on the side of the riverbank, trying to absorb what had just happened.

I didn't know what to say, but I remember muttering, 'thanks,' as I watched little Martha pulling her knees up to her chest, shaking like a leaf.

She knew something really bad had nearly happened, but we were all too relieved to speak.

Tiny Martha had no idea how close she came to drowning that afternoon. I hugged her and tried to make a big fuss, but since we didn't do hugs in our family; she stiffened against my embrace.

After a few minutes of watching and waiting to make sure she was okay, we got dressed and gathered up our stuff. By rights, we should have taken her to the hospital to have her checked out because children can still drown after absorbing water like that, but I didn't know that at the time. We were only kids. We didn't understand any of the risks and were barely able to look after ourselves, never mind each other.

Not being able to swim was a terrible handicap, but none of us ever realised just how much danger we were in.

Playing by the side of a fast-flowing river was like playing with fire, but that's what us kids did back in those days and our parents didn't seemed to care.

Later on that evening, our cousin came over to our house to tell mammy and daddy what had happened in case we got in trouble, but he might as well have been talking to the wall.

My mother looked at my cousin with that 'half-glazed couldn't give a shite expression of hers,' shrugged her shoulders and said nothing.

I knew immediately by my cousin's reaction; he was stunned by this response. Even a 'thank you' might have done, but he wasn't even expecting that, he told me later. It was her 'couldn't care less' attitude that got to him more than anything. He may as well have told her it was raining outside, judging by her reaction, but inwardly, I was fuming. This young boy had saved my sister's life that day and all he got was a shrug.

I was so afraid of what I was going to say next, I had to get up and leave the room. My cousin took that as a cue to leave and followed me towards the front door without saying another word. He was deeply offended by mammy's reaction and I could see it all over his face.

"You horrible, horrible, bitch!" I whispered, under my breath, but I didn't have enough words in my vocabulary to express how I really felt. Today, you might describe her as a vicious, malignant psychotic with the morals of a slice of cheese but that would be a compliment to her and especially if there was food mentioned. You couldn't insult mammy, because she was too stupid to even know she was being insulted, and that was a fact!

I could see my cousin looking at me with that puzzled expression that everyone has whenever they leave our house, but now wasn't the time to explain. I was too annoyed and too embarrassed to say much else.

I didn't want him to go away thinking that we didn't appreciate what he had done, but I knew that's how it looked if mammy was anything to go by.

But he knew what my mother was like before he even stepped in the front door. He just wanted to know how Martha was doing before he left?

I quickly gave him one of those awkward thank you hugs that relatives give on special occasions and shuffled back inside so he wouldn't see me going red.

Next day we were sent back down to the river park as if nothing had ever happened, but I wasn't letting anyone go in the water this time.

ABANDONED AT 11

Saturday was a regular drinking day for mammy and God knows why she made me go along. Whenever I could, I'd meet up with a cousin of mine while mammy went off to flirt with some men in the pub. Mammy had several men on the go we knew about, but there were always a few regulars who kept her topped-up with the drink.

Rumours were flying around about mammy selling herself, but if she was, it can't have been for very much. A glass of Guinness and mammy was anybody's. One lad said to her one day, "are you free?" Mammy said, "no, but I'm reasonable!"

She was unreasonable in every sense of the word and had the morals of an alley-cat. If the conversation didn't revolve around her, she tuned out immediately. You didn't have a conversation with mammy. You just listened. After a half an hour of that, your ears would start to bleed.

As we hung around the square for several hours keeping an eye on the pub, mammy fell out the front door looking the worse for wear.

She was drunk and could barely walk. The only thing that remained upright was the bottle she held tightly in her hand.

"Stella, how come every time I see you, you have a bottle in your hand?" said a woman who lived locally.

"Well, I'm sorry to offend ya missus, but I can't keep it in me fookin' mouth all day? Now where the fook is the chipper?" she said, as she let out a belching roar.

"They won't give me anymore fookin' drink. The fooker behind the bar shez I've had enuff! Can ya fookin' believe that fooker. I'll say when enuff is enuff. No fooker's gonna tell me I've had enuff," she bellowed, as she raised the bottle on top of her head.

"Do I look drunk to youse? Answer me yee pair of cunts?

Do I look drunk... where's de fookin' chipper? I want chips!

Hold on, I need to have a pish. Here, hold that," she said, shoving a bottle of Guinness into my hand.

Mammy turned around and headed back in the door of the pub to the roars and wolf whistles of all the men inside as she swung the door open.

"Ah Jazuz the black Horse is back again, boys. Is it

children's allowance day already? G'wan barman; give that woman another drink before she rides us all."

The comments came fast and furious, and I couldn't decide to follow her back in or stay where I was.

My cousin gave me a nudge, and we half stuck our heads around the corner of the door.

"I'n gonna pish on your floor ya big lanky cunt and I want more drink?" Mammy roared at the barman.

I was mortified and my cousin and I didn't know where to look.

"You can't be listening to this," I said, and urged her to head on home. "Please?" I said. "I don't think either of us should be here?"

My cousin looked at me anxiously and said, "are you sure you'll be okay on your own?"

"I'll be grand," I said, but I really wanted her to stay. Neither of us knew what to do. We had never seen anyone so drunk as this and I was scared out of my wits. What if mammy got in a fight; what if she fell down and hurt herself; what if I couldn't pick her up; who do I call for help? All these questions and more were racing through my mind. My cousin, by now had seen enough and was starting to look upset. A few minutes later, I was left standing by the door on my own.

I felt the whole world was staring at me. I wanted the ground to swallow me up when next minute mammy appeared out of the toilet and made a beeline for the front door.

The men let out another roar, but this time it wasn't so loud because they could see I was getting upset.

I held the door open, and she brushed past me as if I wasn't even there.

"Where's me fookin' bottle of Ginnish yee little cunt?" she says, as I handed it back to her.

A few minutes later, she half fell and half walked through the front door of the chipper and headed straight for the counter, head down.

Only for the height of it, she'd have been straight over the top and into the fryer head first.

The woman and man behind the counter looked at me bemused but didn't say a word. They had seen it all before.

'Fresh cod'n'ships,' slurred mammy, slapping some coins on the counter.

She hadn't ordered for me. She never did, but that was no surprise.

I was hungry. I had nothing to eat all day, and I didn't have any money to get something for myself.

As I looked at her stagger out the door with her dirty fingernails grappling with the bag of chips, I felt a mixture of shame and disgust at the sight of this woman. I was embarrassed, deeply embarrassed. I wanted nothing to do with her but I was too scared to say a thing. I was ashamed. Ashamed to be associated with her because she was everything a mother was not. She was horribly mean and foul-mouthed and she was like that, sober or drunk.

How could I ever show my face in that town again after the carry-on of her in the pub?

All I wanted to do was go home. Whatever she had done to get herself in this terrible state was something I couldn't understand, and now was not the time to start figuring it out.

Minutes later we ended up on the road to try and thumb a lift home when I realised I needed to go to the loo.

"G'wan where you fookin' are," she said.

"I can't! Not on the side of the road?" I said.

"Well, go where you fookin' like, I couldn't give a fook!"

I looked across the road and could see a Library. Maybe I could use the toilet in there!' I said.

"G'wan to fook' she said again, "I'm not waiting around here all day for you to make up your fookin' mind!"

I ran across the road as quickly as I could, but when I got back a few moments later mammy was gone! She had completely disappeared.

I froze with the fright and started to look up and down the road, wondering where she had got herself to.

I stood up on my tippy-toes and tried to look over a hedge next to the field beside the road. Maybe she might have gone to the loo in there, but that didn't make sense. Mammy would have just squatted on the side of the road. She never cared who might be looking at her.

Where could she be? All sorts of possibilities were going through my head. Maybe she followed me over to the Library, wondering what was taking me so long.

That had to be it, so I went back over to take a look. But she was nowhere to be seen. So I went back to the side of the road again and waited and waited for what seemed like an eternity, but after I don't know how long, there was still no sign of her.

I never felt so alone in all my life. I felt completely abandoned and started to cry.

I was only 11-years old on the side of a busy road and my mammy had simply disappeared into thin air.

I was so scared. Maybe she had been abducted. There

had to be a logical explanation for why she had just abandoned me like that?

Not for a second did I think she would go off without me.

The thought she would just leave me there never even crossed my mind. You wouldn't do it to a dog! How could any mother do something as awful as leave her own child on the side of a road?

All these questions were going over and over in my head, and I didn't know what to think.

As luck would have it, I had an aunt who lived nearby, so I quickly made my way over to her house to explain what had happened. When she opened the door, I burst into tears. She was very sympathetic but could offer no explanation for my mother's sudden disappearance.

A phone call was made and we quickly discovered mammy had in fact gotten a lift home without waiting for me. I was so angry. Then, to add to insult to injury, she apparently lied to everyone about what had really happened. She made up some cock and bull story that 'I had been going around town with my cousin Jenny and when it came time to go home, I had refused to go.' That was a horrible lie and I couldn't believe what I was hearing. Mammy had abandoned me on the side of the

road and now here she was, lying through her teeth trying to convince everyone that it was all my fault. I was
so furious I could barely catch my breath.

Even if what she said was true – and that I had actually
done what she said – what right-minded parent would
abandon her own child in the middle of a town?

My Aunt knew by my reaction that mammy was telling
bare-faced lies but she never let on.

"What a dreadful, dreadful, woman," I overheard her
saying to her husband after she put the phone down.

Things went from bad to worse after that. Daddy came
on the phone to say I would be collected tomorrow by
the monster and that I could expect it hot and heavy off
him when I got home.

I burst into tears when I heard this. I had done abso-
lutely nothing wrong to deserve any punishment, and I
cried myself to sleep that night.

When the monster arrived to collect me the following
day, I said goodbye to my aunt and dreaded the thought
of going home.

Instead of heading out onto the main road to thumb a
lift as we always do, he made me follow him up towards
the back of the Library where we couldn't be seen.

I knew immediately what was about to happen. We had

no reason to come up here.

For a moment or two, I wasn't too sure what to do next but when he started to unzip his trousers and told me to lie down, something inside me snapped.

I let out a high-pitched scream at the top of my voice shouting "heeeeellllpppp" as loudly as I could in the hope that someone in one of the houses nearby would hear me.

He looked at me like I had just kicked him in the balls, and his jaw hit the floor. I had never done anything like that before, and he was shocked. The blood had drained from his face and a lot else besides.

He was completely caught unawares and quickly gathered himself up in case someone came.

As he dashed back out onto the road, expecting me to follow, I waited for a brief moment in the hope that someone might turn up. I was in no rush to go and if he decided to leave me there, all the better. I could always go back to my aunt's house where it was safer.

Back on the road, we stood together in silence for what seemed like ages, but inside my heart was still racing. When we eventually got a lift, he hopped into the front as he usually did, and I got in the back. He chatted away to the driver as if nothing had happened, but I was taking none of the conversation in.

I was on an adrenaline high. I was over-flowing with confidence and literally screaming inside.

For the first time ever, I had managed to stop my brother from hurting me and while it was only a small victory; it proved to be a turning point.

For that brief moment, I had found my voice. I realised I could actually make him stop if I wanted to, but unfortunately it was only a brief respite.

SOCIAL WORKERS

I couldn't stomach another bowl of stew. I'd rather starve than eat one more plate of the stuff. Stew in our house was a form of punishment; always in the pot each evening and the same lingering smell. If you didn't eat whatever was on the plate the day before, it was there waiting for you next day until you did. "Ya better eat that ya' spoiled little cunt!" mammy would say. "If you don't, you're going to bed with fookin' nothing in yer stomachs!"

That's fine. I got used to not eating and going to bed hungry was nothing new, but I wasn't going to eat one more plate of stew if my life depended on it.

The next day there was nothing to eat at all. Mammy was found sitting in the corner of the front room with daddy trying to console her. She looked like she had been crying all day and whatever it was; I was determined to find out. Minutes later I discovered the reason for all the upset after talking with one of my sisters. Two social workers had come and gone and given mammy and daddy an ultimatum. Either the boys go or we do? Meaning all the girls would be taken into care if they continued on living in the house.

When I realised both of my brothers had been told to leave, the news stunned me. This couldn't possibly be true? I had never felt so much relief in all my life, but how was this happening and why now, after all these years?

None of this made any sense, but it had to be on foot of a complaint? Social workers are only as good as what they are told and whoever talked was anonymous.

The most likely candidate was my eldest sister, but she never spoke to me about what happened and that still remains the case to this day.

Years later, I discovered she had spoken to several other people, including a priest and the Gardai. When we were approached around the same time as she allegedly made a complaint, I didn't know how to respond and remained silent. I was still living at home at the time and it was impossible to speak up safely in that house. My sister would have known how difficult it was and especially with the monster still there.

Had she approached me personally and told me what she was doing, I think things could have been very different. But this latest development was like a bolt out of the blue. We had no support and no guarantee that if anyone spoke up, anything would be done. We all saw what happened following the rape of our 4-year-old sister. I had no faith in the social workers or Gardai to protect us after that. They had let us down horribly, and we had no reason to trust them, and that remains the case to this day. Taking our two brothers out of the house was too little, too late. One of them should have been removed years earlier, but I can only speak about the monster. Whatever the other one was supposed to have done was a mystery, and I was never told.

A few days later, mammy called me into the kitchen to say the monster had got a job. I was to meet him at 6:30pm on a Friday close to where we lived. My heart sank. She said he had something for her and he only wanted me to collect it. I didn't want to go. I dreaded the thought of seeing that bastard again.

Mammy knew by the look on my face this terrified me. But since when did she ever care? It made no difference to her what he had done. He could have been standing at the end of the road with a chainsaw dripping in blood. And you still had to meet the bastard. That was her mentality. She had the empathy of a postage stamp. I thought to myself, surely the monster wouldn't try anything after being kicked out of the house only a few days earlier? But what if he did? I had in mind to scream even louder than the last time if he so much as touched a hair on my head. I was 13 years-old by this time and while I didn't have his strength; I had a mouth on me like a loud hailer.

When I arrived outside the hotel where we were meant to meet, he was standing on the footpath with a big sheepish head on him. He looked like someone had kicked him up the hole. All the usual cockiness and swagger was gone. Instead, there was this pathetic, slimy creature that looked as if it had slithered out of a drain and someone greased its hair. He stood there staring at me like he mattered, but all I could see was a pig.

The shiny parcel he said was for the mother, and the ice-pops were for us. I didn't trust the bastard for a second. This was the first time he had ever bought anything for anyone, but I never said a word. I just took the lot and walked away.

I knew he was trying to soften me up, but it was going to take a lot more than an ice-pop to lay a hand on me. By that stage, I was so annoyed at having to meet him; I was more likely to kick him in the balls and tear his face off. But I never got the chance. I think he suspected I was about to do exactly that. He had his hands folded over his crotch for the first time ever.

I quickly made my way back up the road as fast as I could. I couldn't get away from him fast enough. Every few steps, I'd look back to see if he was following, but he was gone in the opposite direction.

This was one of a number of gifts he bought for mammy over the following months and every time a neighbour would meet her on the road, her darling son was always the main topic of conversation.

"I got this lovely red necklace from my number one son," she used to say and I felt sick to the pit of my stomach every time she opened her mouth.

Had she any idea the agony that monster had caused? He abused so many children in that house and here she was talking about him like he was the prodigal son.

I wanted to spit. The rage I felt inside me every time she spoke about him was impossible to describe. That horrible piece of shit had raped my 4-year-old sister right in front of my own eyes and I watched in horror as one of my neighbours had to pull him off. Whatever about what he had done to me personally, how could she talk about him in such glowing terms?

How could she talk about him knowing that he belonged in a prison cell for serial rape?

Have you any idea, you stupid, pathetic woman, if you're reading this, how much pain that monster caused?

You horrible, stupid, drunken wretch, you left him with us every single night for years to attack us while you and that other retard were getting shit-faced down the pub? I couldn't look at my mother after that and our relationship quickly started to deteriorate. Not that we had any relationship in the first place, but the abuse from her only began to intensify.

Instead of daddy, she was now blaming me for everything. Her number one son being removed from the home was all my fault, but she never said that to my face. She didn't need to. She had everyone else convinced that it was me and dare anyone tell her otherwise. I was her brand new scapegoat.

Around this time, I had started my first year in secondary school, and I dreaded the thought of coming home each day. All the other girls were talking about boys and makeup and stuff I had no experience of that. I felt totally disconnected from everyone around me.

Whenever a question came up in class, I couldn't concentrate on anything long enough to remember what the teacher had said, and it always got me in trouble.

"Lorraine, are you listening?"

"Yes, miss!"

"What did I just ask?"

"I dunno, miss, I didn't hear you?"

She would only look, but never took me to one side or tried to punish me. Maybe she could see the signs. Maybe she knew what was going on at home?

Kids don't lack concentration for anything.

But had she known the full extent of what was happening, what was she supposed to do; talk to mammy? Nobody talked to mammy. You might as well have a conversation with a chimpanzee?

The subjects I preferred involved doing rather than listening. Home economics, chemistry or art. That sort of thing. Anything that required me to concentrate for longer than thirty seconds put my head in a spin.

I was suffering from emotional overload. The last few years had taken its toll. The weight of keeping things a secret for so long had worn me down. It was obvious what was happening. I had all the symptoms of PTSD (Post-traumatic-stress-disorder) but nobody knew what that was back then.

How I walked, talked and behaved was all part of a

gradual deterioration in mood and I was all over the place. My school uniform provided the perfect cover. For that few hours each day, I was like everyone else, but you didn't have to dig too far to see what was really going on below the surface.

I was a psychological mess. I was never clean; my hair was always matted and rarely washed; my clothes smelled awful and I looked like I felt. I was totally depressed and felt completely detached. But nobody could see that. Those who did, pretended not to, because it raised all sorts of awkward questions nobody wanted to ask.

When I talked earlier about our 5-year-old sister shoving a pencil inside herself in the middle of our street, that should have been an instant red flag for anyone? Why would an innocent child do something as blatant as that and not feel embarrassed? That's not normal? Overly sexualised children only behave like that for a reason and you don't have to look too far for answers. Why didn't social services pick up on that? It wasn't as if the neighbours hadn't told them. Our parents were the last people to tell.

A friend of mine related how another one of my 9-year-old sisters offered to have sex with her 5-year-old son.

When she heard this, she immediately confronted my father. She was livid, but he had nothing to say.

She confirmed the incident in an interview with the journalist writing this book, but it was another stark illustration of what was happening in that house of horrors, and social services were complicit.

When the monster was sent to live with our grand-parents, it didn't take him long to settle in and wreak havoc on the sleepy town where they lived.

The first of his new victims was a cousin of mine, fol-lowed by her brother. The details of what had happened to them were immediately covered up. A sister of my mother made sure of that. Reputation was clearly more important to her than her children being abused.

But when another victim came forward with similar alle-gations of abuse, the pressure began to mount.

I mentioned earlier in the book about a man dragging him down the street in his underwear to the local Garda Station. The father of the little girl he molested showed enormous restraint and his words to the arresting Gardai were, "you do something about him or I will?"

But that never happened and how he is still roaming free to this day, will be explained at the end of this book.

MAN NEXT DOOR

Rumours had been flying around the town that our younger sister Imelda resulted from an affair mammy had with the man next-door. Mr Benson had lived beside us for as long as I could remember and kept himself to himself. Other than the usual pleasantries, he had little to say, but mammy used to talk to him a lot.

Apparently, he was estranged from his British wife, who had returned to England several years earlier. She left him after a short time, but nobody ever knew why? Mammy's name was mentioned, but at the time we were too young to understand what that meant.

Her indiscretions were already the talk of the town. But then one day, somebody let the cat out of the bag and the whole street went into a huddle.

One neighbour said, mammy was getting £40 maintenance a week for Imelda on top of her usual mickey money, as it was known back then. It was a crude derogatory term used to describe women who got pregnant to get children's allowance.

That was a shocking thing to say in such a small town, even if it was true. But nobody dared say it to mammy's face directly. She'd tear the face off them.

I overheard one neighbour saying to mammy during an argument, "Stella don't you fookin' accuse me or my mudder' of sayin' nothin' about you. She told me that you told her what I told you not to tell her. I told her, not to tell you I told her. Well, don't tell her that I told you that she told me is what I'm trying to fookin' tell you; d'ya understand that?"

Nobody understood any of it; but that's the way they talked around where we lived. It was pure word salad. You could never figure out who was saying what, and if you did, you were a retard?

Daddy obviously didn't suspect a thing, and if he did, he never let on.

To look at her, Imelda was the spit of Mr Benson next door; but that didn't tell us very much. There was no such thing as DNA testing in those days and even if there was, mammy couldn't be arsed.

She'd say, "yee may as well get the whole lot of yourselves tested because there's none of yee take after me in this house? I don't remember me last ride, never mind what he looked like, so yee can fook off the lot of yee!"

When Mr Benson died of cancer several years later, he left his house to my sister Imelda, along with €10,000 in cash. His former wife, who failed in her bid to overturn the will and returned to England empty-handed later, contested this. Imelda never saw any of that money or the house either, but it left a lot of unanswered questions that still linger to this day.

Following my departure from the house of horrors, I set about trying to recover from some of the most horrific experiences imaginable. Sometimes I used to pinch myself that I managed to escape at all.

Getting back to anything resembling a normal life again was the hardest thing imaginable. I felt like a prisoner of war and the beatings and constant abuse had left me traumatised. Getting accustomed to normal everyday activities was like learning to walk again, and even that proved difficult. How much emotional damage I had suffered was impossible to know, but I was determined to work through the pain.

Even simple things, like turning a light on and off in my room, was a novelty. Taking a bath was another. Sometimes I would spend the entire morning in the bath just playing with the bubbles and allowing the water from the tap to trickle over my feet.

I didn't think I would ever get clean again. But this cleansing process could never erase some of the terrible nightmares I suffered for weeks and years afterwards. Some nights I would wake up in a cold sweat tearing at the sheets. I would scream out so loudly that my husband would jump out of the bed looking to see who had broken into our room. Sometimes I couldn't sleep at all. My abuser used to come for me at night when I was at my most vulnerable, and that was the most terrifying part of living in that house of horrors.

Sleep, whenever it came, was always disturbed. For the first few years of my marriage, I never closed my eyes for more than a few minutes. If it was pitch black in my room I panicked; I always needed a light on. I became hyper-vigilant. At night I developed an acute sense of hearing and was on constant alert. Even the slightest noise put me on edge. My husband moving barefoot across the bedroom floor could wake me up immediately. I trusted none of these sounds, and as a child, I couldn't figure out if they were footsteps or rodents. In reality, they were one and the same thing. There was no distinction to be made between my abuser and the things that scuttled up the walls. Rats or mice were scary, but far less threatening than the monster.

I had to learn to trust people all over again. Everyone was a potential threat to me and my children.

To keep my mind occupied, I learned to clean. I loved going around with a brush or a cloth and the scruffier the surface, the better. Even the dog wasn't safe. I could see dirt everywhere. I was so angry I didn't know what to do with all of those pent-up emotions, but getting out the bleach or mop was the perfect release.

Later on, when I had more kids, I learned to ease up. Cleaning with kids around is like brushing your teeth and eating biscuits at the same time.

Buying proper food was next. I loved cooking and going around a supermarket was my favourite thing ever. I liked the idea of being able to pick what I liked, and grocery shopping was just another form of therapy. I squeezed everything and especially the bread.

I couldn't stand hard bread. It had to be feather pillow squishy, and I knew why, of course, but I didn't care. I swore I would never eat another stale slice of bread again for the rest of my life.

A new neighbour had moved in beside where we lived

and it wasn't long before we became close friends. He wasn't your typical type of next-door neighbour and when I first met him; I thought he looked a bit stuck up. Initially, we didn't know what to make of him, but as the family got to know him, he wasn't like that at all. But one thing became clear, he knew a lot more about the law than we did and it turned out to be a blessing. He looked and talked like a Guard and when we found out he was an investigative journalist, I couldn't believe my luck. When my husband told him the story of what happened to me, he was shocked and very apologetic. "Someone has let your wife down very badly," was the first thing he said, and he couldn't understand, based on my evidence, why my case had never come to court. "Something just isn't quite right about this," he said. "I've seen cases with flimsier evidence successfully prosecuted and this one just doesn't add up."

He said my brother should have been locked up years ago and all the children being left in that house for as long as they were was shocking beyond belief. 'It made no sense at all?'

I showed him all the notes that I had made, as I had kept a diary over the years, and the more he listened, the more annoyed he became. I explained how I felt totally let down by the justice system and that this missing piece of the jigsaw; the Guards kept referring to, had me confused. He said he would make some enquiries and draw up a list of people to speak to. We subsequently added several members of my family to his list, but only a few agreed to talk.

Initially, they did not know who he was, but it didn't take them long to find out. He said he wanted to hear their side of the story before reaching any conclusions. Most of it was a repeat of what was already said to the Guards, but he uncovered fresh evidence that was about to blow a hole in the original investigation.

Following my first complaint, he discovered that several key witnesses (4 sisters) had been corralled together into one-room to give their statement to the investigating Gardai.

"That discovery alone, was enough to destroy your case. Interviewing several witnesses together gave them the perfect opportunity to corroborate their stories, so they all matched. It made no sense to do that, and I can't see the logic behind it, unless someone was trying to make this go away?" he added.

"That was gross incompetence by the investigating Garda, and she knew full well what she was doing. You don't shove crucial witnesses all into the one room when you're looking to gather statements. It's common sense. "Unfortunately, the Gardai tend to attract even bigger gougers than the ones they're supposed to go after and there's even more shocking news," he said. "But I think you need to sit down for this one."

I looked at him as he paused, and was dreading what was about to come next.

"I was talking to an ex-Garda in one pub locally following a tip-off. He told me your father used to play darts with the detective who investigated the complaint against your brother. That might explain why the evidence in this case has mysteriously disappeared?"

John Hannigan, who saw my 4-year-old sister being raped, said nothing was ever done about his witness statement. And it would appear Puff the Magic Dragon had burned a big hole in the Garda archives, because it was nowhere to be found.

John Hannigan's evidence, not to mention your own, was sufficient cause for a full investigation into what went on in that house. That should have been launched by the Gardai immediately and social services brought in. All of the children should have been interviewed and properly examined on foot of his testimony, but none of that was done, as we now know?

"This whole case stinks to high Heaven!" he said, as he browsed through his notes. He couldn't believe what he had been told, and neither could we?

"This has all the hallmarks of Garda corruption and I'm not in the least bit surprised they wanted to bury this."

"The Garda Siochanna have a long track record of playing dirty tricks whenever there are allegations of Garda corruption against one of their own.

The likelihood of this case ever making it to court a second time is very slim for that reason but if you want to give it a go, I will help you in any way I can, he said.

"Thank you so much," I said, but I don't understand why you think my chances are slim?"

"Lorraine, I don't want you to get your hopes up, but the Gardai have already contaminated most of the key witnesses in this case, and that's enough to stop it from ever going ahead. The most important witnesses here were your own sisters. They all appear to have been deliberately sabotaged by the Gardai, he said.

Secondly, the original detective who investigated this case is now retired. We can't prove that he made John Hannigan's statement disappear, and it's going to be a challenge to get him into the witness box if this ever goes to court. He's not obliged to make a statement that might incriminate him, but by the sounds of it, he's a right piece of work, and that's putting it mildly.

I can't think of any Garda I know personally that would do what he did. To me, leaving a house full of innocent kids at the mercy of someone like your brother is unconscionable. But that's what appears to have happened in this case. It's one of the most horrendous cases of Garda malfeasance I've ever encountered.

My husband and I looked at each other, shocked.

"What do you think we should do?" I asked.

"I'm really not sure, Lorraine. I don't think you have enough evidence to launch a new investigation just yet. We need more. A lot more! We need one of your sisters to come forward and make a statement because right now it's you against an awful lot of players and we may include the Gardai and Tusla in that.

"What about Imelda?" he said.

"I have no idea where she lives now?" I replied.

"Well, let's see if we can find her. That shouldn't be too difficult. I remember you saying she hates your mother?"

"With a passion! Even more, than I hate her, if that's humanly possible!" I said.

"Let's go for a drive tomorrow. I think I know where to find her. I just don't have an exact address."

This journalist was the only other person, apart from my husband and the Guards, who knew what went on in that house. It was an enormous relief to be finally telling my story after so many years.

He listened carefully to everything I had to say, and he explained, from his perspective, why he thought it was so difficult for me to report what happened. While some of what he has to say may be controversial to some, it might also explain why hundreds of women in Ireland, like myself, found it so difficult to speak up.

"Sexual abuse is never an easy thing to talk about and in Ireland and we have a lot of catching up to do when it comes to the subject of sex. To understand why it was so difficult for women to come forward, we need to look at some of the challenges they faced during the early parts of the last century.

Growing up in catholic Ireland during the 60s and 70s was far removed from the cultural revolution taking place in the US and elsewhere. There was "nun" of that hippy carry-on allowed if you'll excuse the pun. Sex was taboo, and the clerics came out in their droves to condemn all this hedonistic debauchery. Nuns somehow became guardians of morality, and yet what they knew about sex could be written on the back of a postage stamp. These women were married to God which is about the most reliable form of birth control available. The chances of immaculate conception magically re-appearing was equally remote. With so much forensic testing available getting that past a midwife is a big ask. Sex outside of marriage was a mortal sin and so was being left-handed. Only for my father, who was a Guard, and told them to stop, they would have broken my fingers. They'd used to lash me with canes and slam chalk dusters down on my hand in order to get me to use my right. Not only write with it, but picking my nose, raising my hand in class or throwing stones at them, all had to be done with the correct hand. To use your left was a cardinal sin.

I was only 5-years-old at the time, but these demented penguins, were convinced I was an apprentice demon. And there's probably some truth to that, because I've been like a divil with a pen ever since.

That sort of superstitious nonsense is all very well, but as I said to one of them recently, "I'd love to see things from your point of view, but I don't think I could get my head that far up my arse?"

As the religious abuse scandals started to emerge, people began to question these lunatics. Nuns weren't just beating up left-handed kids, they stood accused of unspeakable crimes, and priests the same, but there were no clerical convictions when I was growing up.

They got away with murder – quite literally – and you can understand why. As far as they were concerned, we were all sinners. Sex was for the great unwashed. Parents instinctively felt their kids were safe with these paragons of virtue. Little did we know, some of them turned out to be the most evil bastards on the planet.

If a girl got pregnant outside of wedlock, she was a sinner no matter how the pregnancy came about.

And the nuns pulled on the gloves. They disposed of illegitimate babies in their hundreds and that word alone was a guaranteed death sentence. Children had every legitimate right to exist without prejudice, but not if the mother commited a mortal sin?

It's scandalous what these religious fanatics got away with, and that's still the case to this day. They shoved girls who were sexually abused or pregnant into these baby homes and treated them like vermin.

It was a form of state sanctioned genocide, and children

whose only sin was to be born out of wedlock were among their victims. The church controlled all sexual proclivities within the community and to question their authority risked a mauling from the pulpit. Nobody took a stand against this religious bigotry back in the day. Not even the Gardai. If there was any hint that the local parish priest was being impugned, you were given a stern talking to or a clip on the ear. Priests interfering with young girls or boys, was unheard of. You had to have imagined it or made it up?

These pillars of the community had married half the Gardai in the parish and officiated over baptisms and burials, let's not forget? How could some 12-year-old abuse victim, be believed over a man of the cloth?

If there were too many victims, as we later discovered; the local Bishop had the offender quietly relocated to another parish where they could re-offend and assault more victims in peace. Arresting or jailing these perverts, was simply out of the question.

Today, in the US, over 1,700 priests and other clergy members belonging to the catholic church who stand accused of child sexual abuse are in hiding with little to no oversight from religious authorities or law enforcement. And with good reason. Nobody wants to believe there were that many bastards defiling their children? Religion encourages abuse. When contempt for sex is part of what they teach, this creates the perfect breeding ground for sexual and moral turpitude. If the nuns weren't burying the evidence of girls' so-called crimes against morality, the priests were molesting the survivors. They were loathsome predators who worked hand in glove with each other to conceal their crimes. There wasn't a safe place left in the country if you think about it? If they weren't putting the fear of God in you, they were brainwashing you into believing everything they said and did was right.

Listening to your local parish pillock giving out shite from the pulpit was a regular Sunday rant. These holier-than-thou guardians of morality had far too much to say for themselves. They had little or no life experience following entry into the priesthood, and most of what they preached was straight out of a book of fairy tales.

People are no longer prepared to accept all that rubbish, but that has put a stop to none of them.

Thou shalt not steal, thou shalt not commit murder or covet thy neighbour's wife or rob his TV? Sure that's all common sense? We don't need a priest or the ten commandments to tell us any of that?

People inhabited this earth long before Jesus was ever around. Are we supposed to believe our cave-dwelling ancestors were stuck in purgatory until God turned up a few thousand years later to rescue them all from their sins? And what about this notion that we're all born sinners? What's that about? God gave his only son to die on the cross because of us? Now, hold your horse's right there, as I said to one priest, who started to turn cyanotic with rage. Sure that's an awful guilt bomb to be dropping on any community, never mind impression-able young minds?

Give away who you like, but don't blame that decision making on us. Why should we all go down on bended knees and beg for forgiveness for something we didn't do or had any hand in? According to the bible there's a rake of us up for manslaughter? For what? I didn't nail anybody to a cross? Even posing questions like this is legal blasphemy?

Why should we be punished or threatened with hell and damnation for questioning the logic of that?

That doesn't sound like a very open minded or forgiving God to me? But that's what God demands of us and if you don't do as you're damn well told, you're going to hell?

If that was a parent, social services would take the kids off you, but not if your name is God, it seems?

It's a very Irish way of looking at things, but as I listened to this journalist talk, I knew every word of it made sense.

Now, the Virgin Mary was a different story. I got some comfort from the thought that she was the genuine article. Admittedly, there was a question mark over whether she was as virtuous as the holy book was trying to make out, but you know yourself, you couldn't be asking too many awkward questions in case a few more bubbles got burst.

My next-door neighbour doesn't believe in her either, as if you haven't already guessed? And whenever the subject of religion comes up, that's when the kettle goes on. "There's this antiquated attitude towards sex in Ireland that turns ordinary, intelligent people into gobshites," he says. Many people in rural Ireland have an awful habit of worshipping pieces of plaster and telling tall tales. It's probably a cultural thing, but I haven't quite figured it out. 'Immaculate conception,' or 'immaculate deception,' as I like to call it, is one of the biggest lies ever foisted upon us. How, in the name of Joseph, did Mary manage to get pregnant, without having sex?

I'm not trying to suggest Joseph wasn't up to the job, but don't give me all that miracle nonsense? The only miracle I know comes in a jar and you spread it on crackers. That's about all they have in common. Now, if you ask me, someone wasn't too comfortable with the whole notion of Mary doing the bold thing? And especially outside of marriage? Sure that's a fierce political scandal altogether. They couldn't have that?

Some Greek theologian needed a PR spin before too many of those books were printed. And it makes total sense if you look at their teachings?

Sex to Nuns is an awful filthy thing, and as we all know, the Virgin Mary could never do anything like that.

So, they drafted this cock and bull story and called it 'immaculate conception' to make her look good, and everyone else feel shite. It really is as simple as that! And don't get me started on the loaves and fishes or turning water into wine? That's another bowl of shite!"

"Could you imagine if Moses worked for Tesco's and the money he'd be on? He'd be worth a feckin' fortune and driving a Lambo in the morning?

And what about the 5 loaves and 2 fishes that were supposed to have fed 5,000 with the big hungry heads on them? In fairness, the size of the portions can't have

been that great, but all that shite is in the book!"
Even my own daughter, who was listening to him,
chimed in, "sure, he's right mammy that wouldn't even
feed our family?" she said, laughing out loud.

Deep down, I knew all of this was true but prayer gave
me the strength to get through an awful lot of stuff and
there's no harm in having a few delusions; I said.
"Lorraine, growing up in catholic Ireland during the
'70's meant you were guilty before you were even born.
And that guilt weighs heavily on you for the rest of your
life. If more people weren't made to feel so bad about
sex, I think speaking up would have been a lot easier
and more perverts like your brother might be in jail.
How is a child supposed to report abuse if it already
feels ashamed? The church has a lot to answer for and
so do the courts when you think about it? When you go
to court you have to swear on the Bible to tell the truth,
the whole truth, and nothing but the truth, so help you
God, but what if it's full of lies as I've already dis-
cussed? Nobody wants to hear that, but that holy book
is supposed to represent the truth when in fact, it's
packed full of biblical nonsense? How is anyone supposed to have faith in a justice system that can't distin-
guish between fact and fiction? And the Gardai, who

you are supposed to trust, are not much better. Some of them are so crooked they can't lie straight in bed, but we'll come back to them later," he said.

DEAR SUPERINTENDENT

Thursday 15th November 2017

I wish to make a formal complaint on two counts. 1) In relation to Garda ____ _____ who I met with on 1st of Nov 2017. This was in relation to a case of abuse she was investigating on my behalf and new evidence uncovered by me in relation to that case. I was given several assurances that this new evidence would be investigated promptly given the very serious nature of this complaint. That evidence related to a statement given by a former neighbour of mine, ____

_____, who witnessed a rape of my sister _____
_____ by my brother _____ _____ during the late
1980s on a date unknown.

Following the meeting with Garda _____ _____ I was
given several verbal assurances that she would phone
me back promptly to give me an update on progress.
No phone calls were returned.

I made two follow-up phone calls myself to *****
Garda station following the meeting on the 1st November. Neither of which were returned.

I made a 2nd phone call at 20:59 on the 7th November,
to ***** Garda station requesting to speak with Garda
_____ _____. I was informed that she was on duty but
not available and the Garda would take a message and
pass it on.

I was deeply upset by the fact that that phone call was
also NOT returned notwithstanding the fact that I was
in possession of critical new evidence that should have
been followed up on promptly. I am making this complaint without prejudice and have no further comment
to make at this time.

GARDA STATION

I wasn't about to be kept waiting around a second time. I rang the buzzer on the Garda station door and a male Garda appeared behind the counter and said, 'can I help you?'

'Yes, I'd like to speak to the Sergeant on duty?' I said.

'What's this about?' said the Guard.

'I'd like to make a complaint in relation to a case being handled by a Garda Sheila McLoughlin and I need to speak with the Sergeant on duty please?'

'Hang on,' he said, and I'll see if he's available.'

The guard disappeared through another door and re-appeared a moment or two later.

'He's in a meeting and won't be available for another hour. Can I take your number and get him to call you?'

'You can,' I said, and he jotted down my mobile on a pad in front of him.

'Do you think I can expect a call by today?' I asked the guard as I made my way towards the exit.

'Yes, he'll call you by the end of the day,' he replied.

I didn't believe a word of it. Two weeks earlier and several phone calls later, I'd been promised the same thing and no phone calls were ever returned. There was a pattern to this.

When I eventually met with Garda McLoughlin, I explained to her that I had uncovered new evidence in relation to my case and there were one or two questions bothering me that needed to be clarified.

I informed her I had recently met with a former neighbour of mine, John Hannigan, who had witnessed one of my sisters being abused. His statement to social workers and Gardai at the time appeared to have gone missing.

His testimony was a vital piece of evidence and was potentially the missing piece of the puzzle that Garda

McLoughlin had talked about earlier.

What John Hannigan had seen my brother doing to my sister that day should have been investigated.

His testimony confirmed what I had been saying all along.

My brother was raping us and I couldn't understand how his evidence had suddenly disappeared.

Only for a family friend, none of this would have come to light. He also uncovered some explosive new evidence which warranted a reopening of the original investigation.

My father had played darts with several members of the Gardai who used to meet up in the local pub.

Jack Donegan, a retired Garda who was living locally and tasked with investigating my family, was one of them.

Why was Garda Donegan allowed take a statement from my father if he knew him socially? Surely that was a conflict of interests right there?

Was Donegan not obliged to let his superiors know he knew my father personally? Anyone with a shred of common sense would know that he shouldn't have been allowed within a thousand yards of this case.

I put all of this to the Guard sitting across the desk and

she looked like she was about to say something and then hesitated.

We stared at each other for what seemed like an eternity, but no sounds were coming out. I was visibly frustrated, and she knew by the look on my face that I was getting upset.

'Should I just stop asking questions?' I said.

'No, no, carry on,' she said. 'I just don't have any answers for you at this moment and I'd prefer to talk to you on your own.'

I had brought along a friend with me for moral support and when he heard what the Guard said; he stood up, excused himself and left the room without saying a word.

Now there were just the two of us left.

'I didn't want to answer you Lorraine, because I was worried he might be recording me.'

'Oh,' I said, slightly taken aback.

'Who is he?' she asked.

'He's a close friend of the family,' I said.

'And how do you know him?' she continued.

I felt like saying, 'that's none of your business,' but thought better of it. I didn't want to come across rude but I knew what she was trying to get at.

Her line of questioning was irritating, and I was becoming increasingly frustrated. As far as I was concerned, this was just a distraction from more important questions that needed answering and who he was, was irrelevant. The fact that she knew he was a journalist was obviously what she was trying to get at, but that was her problem, not mine. I wanted to get to the bottom of this.

'And what about John Hannigan's statement; what's going to happen about that?' I asked.

'Yes!' she said, pausing for a moment to fiddle with some papers. 'I'm going to have to bring that to the attention of my Sergeant and come back to you if that's okay?'

'I'm really surprised that his statement was not brought to the attention of the DPP (Director of Public Prosecutions)?'

'Well, as you know, John Hannigan wouldn't give us another statement?'

"And who could blame him," I said. What was wrong with his original statement and where had that got to? She didn't reply.

Like me, John Hannigan was furious about how things turned out. All of my sisters should have been taken out of that house on the strength of his evidence, and the Gardai going back to this man a second time was nothing short of an outrage. Nothing had been done the first time and all of it was just too little, too late, as far as he was concerned.

He was angry with the Gardai, but not half as much as I was. Where was the follow-up? Where was the protection we so desperately deserved at the time?

How could anyone let children stay in a house with a monster like that and not do something about it?

John Hannigan had given a sworn statement that a child was being raped in that house. He had seen it with his own eyes.

John says he remembers the day vividly when I came to him screaming for help for my 4-year-old baby sister. He said, 'he ran up the stairs of the house and saw my brother on top of Helen on the bed and the rest is too graphic to go into here. But there was no doubt in anyone's mind about what he witnessed.

John said, when I grabbed him to shove him down the stairs, he started to fuck me out of it and everything else.'

I told your mother and father the following day, 'when yee are going out again you need to keep an eye on that lad.'

When questioned about the incident at a later date, John Hannigan told the Guards and social services, 'those kids shouldn't be there,' and that's exactly what he said to them.

Why was there nothing done about this when it was first reported and why were the Guards now coming looking for a new statement after all this time?

On the strength of John's evidence, an immediate investigation should have been launched. His testimony could have put a stop to what had happened to us all, but nothing was ever done. Why not? Can someone answer me that?

As I walked out of the Garda station that day I said to my husband, standing outside "surely to God, this can't be happening all over again?"

I felt like the Gardai weren't listening at all, and I was fuming. I was 43-years-old by that time, and I wanted my life back. Those inside were about to discover just how determined I was to get justice. They were in for a rude awakening. I wasn't a child anymore, and I wasn't prepared to tolerate anymore cover-ups or blue-collar lies.

The gloves were off. Whatever goodwill existed between

me and the Gardai was well and truly gone.

I had suffered far too much because of their ineptitude, and when the investigation was reopened, I couldn't believe my ears. Finally, some hope I thought, but incredibly after more months of waiting and investigating, I got the exact same result. Two Gardai sat in my front room, looking embarrassed as they delivered the news. Despite over 30 witnesses prepared to come forward, including a brand new statement from John Hannigan, there was insufficient evidence for the DPP to proceed, they said. I was stunned, but not really surprised at the same time. This time I was prepared. I knew the level of corruption and the damage done to my sister's statements would impact my chances of going to court, but it didn't make it any less painful.

A GSOC investigation that followed into allegations of Garda corruption proved inconclusive. That all important missing statement still couldn't be found and the original detective involved in my case had long since retired. But this fight isn't over. Not by a long shot! There is a monstrous predator still on the loose, and I am determined more than ever to put him behind bars. My parents might be protecting him, but this time I'm not alone. I know from speaking to others on social media there are countless others who have suffered similarly. This book is for you too, and I hope it brings you some comfort. Never, ever, give up the fight and I'll talk to you all soon.

Love and hugs,
Lorraine x

EDITOR'S COMMENT

On the face of it, this case is arguably one of the worst miscarriages of justice I've ever encountered in all my years as a journalist. Not just because of the number of victims involved, but the sheer volume of evidence gathered in this case.

Following Lorraine's decision to publish her story, her family shunned her, and this only fueled her determination to succeed. Her parents have painted her as a liar throughout this entire investigation, despite overwhelming evidence to the contrary. The fact that they were complicit in covering up many of the alleged crimes might explain much of that hostility, but that's an inevitable consequence of telling the truth. Lorraine, understandably, has severed all contact with them in favour of justice and remains undeterred.

Following a second Garda investigation, I attempted to encourage some of her sisters to come forward, but except for one possible witness, none of them did.

Her parents have failed in their bid to break her spirit,

and she has pursued her abuser despite them. What they put her through was simply horrific. Her treatment in that house of horrors was so traumatic it will no doubt affect her for the rest of her life. She experienced problems with her health and struggles to sleep each night. She suffers constant flashbacks and lives in a permanent state of dread. Lorraine often said she would rather die than go through what she did again, but there's little or no chance of that. She felt there was nobody she could talk to about what happened, and her husband did whatever he could to help. He could do little to shed light on what these people had done to his precious wife, and he too is a victim based on the evidence. Lorraine's testimony was heart-breaking, and all I could feel was a growing sense of anger at the injustice of it all. This was a woman who wouldn't hurt a fly. And a more gentle and caring soul you could not meet. The idea of anyone raising a hand to Little Lorraine, as the title of this book suggests, is impossible to imagine once you meet her. Lorraine has this lovely bubbly personality that endears her to everyone. In stark contrast to the parents she was raised by, she is a gentle, kind mother who can't do enough for people and for that reason, she is vulnerable. By her own admission,

she still finds it hard to assert herself and say no.
But if that's the case today as an adult, one can only
imagine how it was for her as a child?

We will probably never know what possessed her parents to behave the way they did and why they abandoned their children each night to be ravaged by a serial
predator. They knew full well what he was doing and
even with all the publicity surrounding this case; they
have made no attempts to come forward and give their
side of the story. If anything, they have frustrated all attempts to uncover the truth and you may include the
Gardai and social workers in that summary as well.

And that's why this book is so important. It is a desperate attempt by one woman to seek justice against a system that has failed her. Her right to be heard cannot be
ignored. Lorraine characterises her parents as the most
despicable people she has ever met in her life.

The home she grew up in was a toxic environment
mired in scandal; plagued by secrets that every one of
her sisters knew about, but nobody dared reveal. The
fear of being tortured or fostered, or shunned if you
spoke out, was ever present.

The spirit of almost every one of the girls in that house
had been broken. They were like tiny ghosts who had

no choice but to maintain their vow of silence.

Thirty-odd years later, the relationship between Lorraine and her parents is completely diminished. It went from ambivalence to total estrangement in a matter of years. But something else happened that her parents didn't expect. They could sense Lorraine's detachment as she grew in strength. The people that now surround her are far removed from the toxic influences she grew up with. Nobody should ever be punished for speaking the truth, but to accuse Lorraine of lying was arguably their most egregious mistake.

After talking with Lorraine over countless hours, I needed no convincing she was telling the truth. And there were other victims besides who had suffered at the hands of this depraved predator. All of them had similar stories to tell. I spoke to several of them personally, and their stories were harrowing.

As a journalist, you have an obligation to remain impartial, but Lorraine's case will provoke public outrage and this book is a distillation of everything learned from talking to those involved in her case.

What this case highlights, is a deeply dysfunctional system of justice that favours the accused and punishes its victims. Several attempts to get Lorraine's abuser into court have been largely unsuccessful and the reasons for that will become apparent, when you read the letter I wrote to a Superintendent on Lorraine's behalf.

During a telephone conversation, he indicated he was prepared to revisit the file and examine the evidence afresh. While he made no promises about any potential outcome, it was a step in the right direction. For the purposes of confidentiality and to avoid prejudicing any future investigations, names have been removed and information redacted.

Dear Superintendent ******,

The facts of this case are as follows: Lorraine McDonagh, made a complaint that *********** ******** had raped and abused her over a period of 4 years starting the day before her communion when she was 8-years-old. For the purposes of expediency, I will not go into the details of her complaint as all of her testimony is a matter of record.

In a recent development, the HSE are on record as saying her allegations "were believable." (see exhibit overleaf) and while their findings are welcome, it doesn't explain how the abuse of Lorraine and her siblings was allowed to go on for as long as it did.

Following my own investigations, several other victims of abuse by the same individual have come forward. Most of *********** ********'s alleged victims, estimated to be over 15 in total, are either too frightened or the probative value of their testimony has been rendered moot by witness intimidation or Garda malfeasance.

I discovered several key witnesses (Lorraine's sisters) had been corralled into one room to provide joint statements. This was told to me by ******* ********, and both myself, Lorraine and her husband, will testify to that. It was a shocking discovery and the ramifications of that left us speechless. This not only flies in the face of standard Garda procedures, but if ever you needed a way to completely destroy a case, look no further than Garda *** ********.

Allowing vital independent witnesses to contaminate each other was not only an act of stupefying incompetence, it made no sense to me whatsoever?

Any prospect of Lorraine taking a case against her abuser hinged on gathering independent statements from each of those witnesses. Garda ******** was aware of that fact and if she wasn't, she had no business wearing a uniform.

To date, Garda ********, has refused to comment on that incident and so did Superintendent ******, at the time. From an evidential point of view, it made little or no sense to do what she did, but not if we probe deeper.

Someone was clearly protecting someone here. Not just Garda members, past and present, but social workers as well.

Social workers like ***** ****** who was aware of a historical complaint by *** ********, and, along with the rest of her colleagues, failed to act on several other pieces of testimony provided by Lorraine's sister ********, and I quote:

"We all know what went on in that house" she said in a recent message to one of Lorraine's facebook friends and former neighbours, ******* ****.

That same neighbour talked about how ******** at the age of 9-years-old invited her 5-year-old boy at the time to have sex with her, but ********, has consistently re-fused to cooperate with the Gardai.

The statement taken from *** ******** who witnessed ********'s rape and its subsequent disappearance has never been fully explained. There was no questioning the veracity of his testimony, but why nothing was done about it demands an explanation.

According to one witness I interviewed, the father of the alleged abuser *********** ********, fraternised with several Birr Garda members who lived locally and regularly met up for darts tournaments. One of those members was former detective ******* *******, who led the initial investigation and took *** ********'s statement.

I was told this by a former Garda member during a chance encounter and I will invoke journalistic privileges to protect that source.

"Any investigation of child abuse that had implications for that member involved was almost certain to fail," he said.

It was a shocking statement, but a serious indictment of the level of corruption that existed within an Garda Siochanna at the time, and, as we know, still continues to this day.

A separate investigation by the Garda Ombudsman, into why *** ********'s statement mysteriously disappeared, has proved inconclusive. The fact that a senior member of GSOC, is allegedly married to a social worker involved in this case shouldn't come as a surprise, but it all leads to one incontrovertible conclusion. This whole case stinks!

Third time lucky was little more than a stark illustration of why the Gardai should never be allowed to investigate their own.

Those same Gardai, who were guilty of contaminating

witnesses back in 2014, were back in the fray and tasked with spearheading a 'new' tax-payer funded inquiry.

I was dumbfounded. A letter of complaint was submitted to your predecessor, and the two Gardai cited in that complaint were subsequently removed from the case.

In hindsight, it was a pyrrhic victory. The damage done to Lorraine's case was like trying to walk on a severed spine. The fact that the Gardai managed to paralyse this case, not once, but twice, seems extraordinary, but the evidence will speak for itself.

For Lorraine, her ordeal is the final denouement in a case that has left a trail of unanswered questions and most of them have been ignored by Birr Gardai.

Superintendent ****** ******, having re-opened the investigation, arguably gave it his best shot, but you can't re-cork a bad bottle of wine. All the key witnesses were beyond recovery and *** ********'s statement, along with her abuser, still remains at large.

Asking *** ******** to resubmit a statement that was given over 30 years prior was preposterous, and the Gardai knew that. Why his testimony wasn't acted upon at the time infuriated the man, and quite rightly so. He was prepared to go up against a whole community in

Birr at the time, but the most damning aspect of this whole case is the damage and destruction caused to so many lives as a direct result of Garda neglect and malfeasance.

But this is no witch hunt. The vast majority of Gardai do an extremely difficult job with honesty and integrity but those directly involved in this case have a professional, if not moral obligation, to explain themselves. Anyone who questions this narrative need only look at the lessons learned from whistle-blowers like Sgt Maurice McCabe. Some of the most senior members of an Garda Siochanna were little more than common criminals, and unfortunately, the Gardai are now back in the spotlight once more.

Admittedly, the Gardai cannot be held responsible for what happened at No.* ********, Birr, but that's not in question here. What is in question is why they failed under oath to protect Lorraine and her siblings from further harm and abuse?

They were aware, following *** ********'s original complaint, *********** and ******** ******** were doing little or nothing to protect their own children. So why was no protection order made or sought? Why did the Gardai, on foot of *** ********'s complaint not seek to have the children taken into temporary custody or at the very least examined?

These are questions you clearly cannot answer, but the Gardai failed in their duty and they failed miserably and are continuing to do so is my point.

Lorraine suffered the worst depravity imaginable and there has been no apology sought nor any given.

But to reopen the same investigation, knowing the damage that was done to vital witnesses, seems an incredibly capricious and cruel thing to do.

On the face of it, this case should never have got to this stage. Her abuser should never have been allowed to continue his reign of terror and the fact that he continues to walk free to this day is largely as a result of Garda failures.

A chance encounter by a neighbour who witnessed Lorraine's 4-year-old sister being raped was more than enough evidence to warrant his immediate arrest, but somehow, it did the complete opposite. Instead, all it told us was vital statements can suddenly disappear at the drop-of-a-hat!

When another investigation was launched in 2014, it was a golden opportunity to put things right. Having failed Lorraine so miserably the first time, you'd be forgiven for thinking the Gardai would get it right.

They ought to have recognised one of their own ex-members should never have been allowed near the case and when several key witnesses were corralled into one room, that only added insult on top of historical injury. How can you explain that?

There are some very uncomfortable questions gathering around Superintendent ******'s role during that whole investigation, but since he is now retired, we are unlikely to ever get a full and frank explanation.

The fact that a member on his watch allowed vital witnesses to contaminate each other was not only an act of egregious incompetence, it was clearly deliberate.

When *** ******** witnessed what he did back in the 1980s, the investigating detective – who knew Lorraine's father both personally and socially – should have re-cused himself immediately. The fact that he did not, is a central feature of this case.

Young, innocent girls were left to suffer horrendous vi-olations, and their brother continued to rape and abuse them with impunity.

How ********** ******** managed to get away with what he did is clearly a matter for the courts, but I sub-mit, it was partly a failure by an Garda Siochanna to self-regulate and this is the thrust of Lorraine's complaint. Any lingering doubts that this was her word against his, is totally misguided. Much of the evidence in Lorraine McDonagh's case is anecdotal but we cannot ignore the volume of it and her continued attempts to seek justice. This is shaping up to be one of the worst serial abuse cases in the history of the state.

A large social media campaign has been launched and a series of protests are planned that will be asking why so many children were allowed to suffer needlessly?

I don't have the answers to those questions. [END]

It is clear from the evidence in this case, the Gardai not only failed in their duty of care to Lorraine and her sisters, they failed numerous other victims as well. There was no legitimate excuse for allowing this predator to continue his reign of terror, and the fact that is he still walking free to this day is nothing short of an outrage. This book is a testimony to Lorraine's strength, courage, and unwavering determination to put him behind bars and her campaign for justice continues.

All the proceeds from this book will go towards helping other victims of abuse and if you would like to lend your support, please visit:

www.justiceforlorraine.com

USEFUL LINKS

If you have been affected by any of the information contained in this book, the numbers provided below may be of some assistance. Please also consider leaving a review on Amazon or social media if you think this book will prove helpful to others.

Rape Crisis Support
Call free: 1800 77 8888
www.drcc.ie

Childline
Call free: 1800 66 66 66
www.childline.ie

Pieta House
Call free: 1800 247 247
www.pieta.ie

Printed in Great Britain
by Amazon

63535550R00139